THE XXL SOUP MAKER RECIPE BOOK

Over 100 Days of Delicious and
Nutritious Recipes for Your Soup Maker
- Quick, Easy and Super-Delicious
Meals for Every Day Enjoyment

AVA MACKENZIE

TABLE OF CONTENTS

Meat Soup Maker Recipes

Superfood Soup Maker Recipes

EXCLUSIVE BONUS

40 Weight Loss Recipes

&

14 Days Meal Plan

Scan the QR-Code and receive
the FREE download:

Soup, the age-old comfort food, has held a special place in our hearts and kitchens for centuries. Whether it's a warm bowl of chicken noodle soup on a chilly day or a hearty vegetable stew that warms your soul, soup has the power to soothe, nourish, and delight.

But what if we told you there's a kitchen gadget that can make soup preparation faster, easier, and more convenient than ever? That's where the soup maker comes into play.

In this comprehensive guide to soup makers, we'll dive deep into the world of these incredible appliances.

From understanding what a soup maker is to selecting the right one for your needs, learning how to use it, and exploring a wide array of delectable soup recipes, we've got you covered.

By the end of this guide, you'll be a soup maker pro, ready to create culinary comfort in your kitchen.

CHAPTER 1:
WHAT IS A SOUP MAKER?

1.1 DEFINITION AND OVERVIEW

A soup maker is a kitchen appliance designed to simplify the process of soup preparation. It combines the functions of a blender and a heating element in one device, allowing you to effortlessly create delicious soups, stews, and purees.

Soup makers come in various shapes and sizes, but they all share the same basic principles: they blend, heat, and cook your ingredients to perfection, often in a single pot.

1.2 TYPES OF SOUP MAKERS

There are primarily two types of soup makers available in the market:

1.2.1 BASIC SOUP MAKERS

Basic soup makers have a single blending and heating chamber. They are straightforward to use and suitable for making a wide range of soups. These models are typically more affordable and user-friendly, making them an excellent choice for beginners.

1.2.2 MULTIFUNCTIONAL SOUP MAKERS

Multifunctional soup makers offer a wider range of features and capabilities. They may include additional settings for sautéing, steaming, or even making smoothies and purees. While they provide more versatility, they are often pricier and may have a steeper learning curve.

1.3 BENEFITS OF USING A SOUP MAKER

Why should you consider adding a soup maker to your kitchen arsenal? Here are some compelling reasons:

In the fast-paced world of modern cuisine, where time is often a precious commodity, kitchen appliances that can save time and effort while delivering delicious results are highly sought after. The soup maker is one such kitchen innovation that has gained popularity in recent years. But what are the benefits of using a soup maker, and why should you consider adding one to your kitchen arsenal? In this section, we will explore the compelling reasons that make a soup maker a valuable addition to any home cook's toolkit.

1.3.1 Time-Saving Convenience

In our busy lives, convenience is key when it comes to meal preparation. Soup makers are renowned for their ability to streamline the soup-making process, significantly reducing the amount of hands-on cooking time required. Traditional soup-making methods often involve multiple steps, from chopping ingredients to monitoring cooking times and temperatures. With a soup maker, you can say goodbye to these laborious tasks.

The convenience of a soup maker lies in its simplicity. Most models come equipped with preset programs for various types of soups, such as smooth soups, chunky soups, and even specific recipes like tomato bisque or butternut squash soup. These preset programs are designed to take the guesswork out of soup preparation, ensuring that your soups turn out perfectly every time.

Using a soup maker is as easy as adding your ingredients, selecting the appropriate program, and pressing a button. The machine takes care of the rest, including chopping, cooking, and blending. The result? A piping hot, homemade soup ready to enjoy in as little as 20-30 minutes, with minimal effort on your part. Say goodbye to hours spent stirring pots on the stove and hello to more free time for yourself.

1.3.2 Effortless Operation

One of the standout features of soup makers is their user-friendly design. These appliances are specifically engineered for ease of use, making them accessible to both experienced and novice cooks alike. You don't need advanced culinary skills to create restaurant-quality soups with a soup maker.

The straightforward operation of a soup maker begins with its intuitive control panel. Most models feature easy-to-understand buttons and digital displays that allow you to choose the type of soup you want to make and adjust settings as needed. Whether you're aiming for a smooth and velvety cream of mushroom soup or a hearty and chunky vegetable stew, the soup maker has you covered.

Beyond the convenience of preset programs and user-friendly interfaces, soup makers often come with additional functions that enhance their versatility. Some models can sauté ingredients like onions and garlic right in the soup maker before proceeding to the cooking and blending stages. This means you can develop rich, layered flavours in your soups without the need for extra pots and pans.

For those looking to expand their culinary horizons, some soup makers can also double as versatile kitchen appliances. These multi-functional units can handle tasks beyond soup-making, such as steaming vegetables for a healthy side dish or blending smoothies and shakes for a quick and nutritious breakfast. This adaptability makes a soup maker a valuable asset in any kitchen, saving both counter space and time.

1.3.3 Versatility

While the name suggests that soup makers are solely dedicated to soup preparation, many of these kitchen gadgets offer a range of versatile functions. Beyond crafting soul-warming soups, these machines can perform various culinary tasks, further adding to their appeal and utility.

1. **Sautéing**: As mentioned earlier, some soup makers come equipped with sauté functions. This feature allows you to brown and caramelise ingredients like onions and garlic before commencing the soup-making process. Sautéing adds depth of flavour to your soups and is a technique commonly used in professional kitchens.

2. **Steaming**: If you're conscious about maintaining the nutritional value of your vegetables, many soup makers can double as efficient steamers. This means you can steam your favourite veggies to perfection, retaining their vibrant colours and essential nutrients. Steamed vegetables make for a healthy side dish or a delightful addition to your soups.

3. **Blending**: Beyond the realm of soups, soup makers excel at blending tasks. Whether you're whipping up a refreshing fruit smoothie, creating a creamy sauce, or preparing a silky puree, these machines can handle the blending process with ease. This versatility extends the range of culinary creations you can craft in your kitchen.

4. **Crushing Ice**: Some soup makers have the capability to crush ice, making them a handy tool for preparing chilled beverages or frosty desserts like frappes or slushies. With the push of a button, you can transform ice cubes into fine, snow-like ice crystals to elevate your refreshments.

1.3.4 Healthier Eating

One of the most significant advantages of using a soup maker is the control it gives you over the quality and nutritional content of your meals. When you make your soups from scratch, you have the power to select the finest ingredients and customise your recipes to suit your dietary preferences and health goals.

Making soup at home allows you to choose fresh, wholesome ingredients. You can select the ripest vegetables, lean proteins, and high-quality stocks or broths. This control over ingredients means you can create soups that are not only delicious but also packed with essential nutrients. You can avoid the excessive sodium, preservatives, and additives often found in store-bought soups, making your meals healthier and more nourishing.

Furthermore, with the ability to customise your soups, you can cater to specific dietary requirements. Whether you're following a low-sodium diet, seeking to reduce your calorie intake, or accommodating food allergies, you can tailor your soup recipes accordingly. The flexibility of a soup maker allows you to create dishes that align with your health and wellness objectives.

1.3.5 Cost-Effective

In today's world, being budget-conscious is a priority for many households. While dining out or purchasing pre-packaged soups may seem convenient, it can often be more costly in the long run. Investing in a soup maker can help you save money while still enjoying delicious, homemade soups.

Preparing soups at home is generally more cost-effective than buying pre-made alternatives. When you make soups from scratch, you can purchase ingredients in bulk, take advantage of seasonal produce, and reduce packaging waste. Additionally, creating large batches of soup means you can enjoy multiple servings and freeze leftovers for future meals, further stretching your food budget.

The cost-effectiveness of using a soup maker extends beyond just soup. As mentioned earlier, many models have versatile functions that allow you to perform a variety of kitchen tasks. By eliminating the need for multiple appliances, you can save on kitchen equipment costs while maximising your culinary capabilities.

In conclusion, the benefits of using a soup maker are numerous and compelling. From the time-saving convenience of quick and effortless soup preparation to the versatility that extends beyond soup-making, these kitchen appliances have become invaluable tools for home cooks. Additionally, the ability to make healthier, customised meals and save on food expenses makes soup makers a wise investment for anyone looking to elevate their culinary experience.

In the next chapter, we'll delve into the process of selecting the perfect soup maker for your kitchen.

CHAPTER 2:
CHOOSING THE PERFECT SOUP MAKER

Selecting the right soup maker is a crucial step on your journey to becoming a soup aficionado. Here's what you need to consider when making your decision.

2.1 SIZE AND CAPACITY

Soup makers come in various sizes, typically measured in litres or quarts. Consider how much soup you'll be making at a time.

If you have a large family or frequently entertain guests, a soup maker with a larger capacity (around 1.5 to 2 litres) may be ideal. For smaller households, a compact model with a 1-litre capacity might suffice.

2.2 POWER AND WATTAGE

The power of a soup maker is measured in watts. Higher wattage generally means quicker heating and blending. However, it's important to strike a balance. A soup maker with excessive wattage may be overkill for simple soups and could result in unnecessary energy consumption.

2.3 BLADE QUALITY

The quality of the blender blades can significantly impact the consistency of your soups. Look for soup makers with durable, stainless steel blades that can effortlessly blend both soft and hard ingredients.

2.4 EASE OF CLEANING

Nobody wants to spend hours scrubbing a complicated appliance after making a batch of soup. Opt for a soup maker with removable, dishwasher-safe parts to make cleanup a breeze.

2.5 ADDITIONAL FEATURES TO CONSIDER

- **Programmable Settings**: Some soup makers offer preset programs for different soup types, making it easier to achieve the perfect consistency and flavour.
- **Keep Warm Function**: This feature keeps your soup warm for an extended period, allowing you to enjoy hot soup whenever you're ready.
- **Safety Features**: Look for safety features like automatic shut-off and anti-scalding protection to ensure worry-free operation.
- **Steamer Baskets**: If you want to steam vegetables or other ingredients for your soup, consider a soup maker with an included steamer basket.

Now that you're equipped with the knowledge to choose the right soup maker, let's move on to the practical aspects of using one.

CHAPTER 3:
GETTING STARTED WITH YOUR SOUP MAKER

3.1 UNBOXING AND INITIAL SETUP

When you first get your soup maker, it's essential to unbox it carefully and read the instruction manual thoroughly. Here's a general outline of what you'll need to do:

- **Unboxing**: Carefully unpack all the components included with your soup maker. Ensure that nothing is damaged during transit.
- **Cleaning**: Before using your soup maker for the first time, wash all removable parts, including the blending jug and lid, with warm soapy water.
- **Power Up**: Place your soup maker on a clean, dry, and level surface near a power outlet. Plug it in and familiarise yourself with the control panel.
- **Initial Test**: Run a test cycle with water to ensure that everything is functioning correctly.

This helps eliminate any factory residues and ensures your soup maker is ready for food preparation.

3.2 SAFETY TIPS AND PRECAUTIONS

While soup makers are generally safe to use, it's essential to follow some basic safety guidelines:

- Never immerse the base of the soup maker in water or any liquid.
- Keep the soup maker away from the edge of the counter to prevent accidental spills.
- Always operate the soup maker with the lid securely in place to prevent hot liquids from splattering.
- Use oven mitts or pot holders when handling the hot soup maker jug or lid.
- Avoid overfilling the soup maker, as this can lead to spills or uneven cooking. Follow the recommended maximum fill line.

3.3 BASIC OPERATING INSTRUCTIONS

Using a soup maker is an uncomplicated process, and most models follow a similar operational pattern. In this section, we will provide you with comprehensive guidance on how to operate your soup maker effectively. Whether you're a seasoned cook or a newcomer to the world of soup makers, these basic instructions will ensure that you get the most out of your appliance.

Prepare Your Ingredients

Before diving into the operation of your soup maker, the first crucial step is to prepare your ingredients. This step sets the foundation for a delectable homemade soup. Here's what you need to do:

Wash, Peel, and Chop

Start by thoroughly washing all the vegetables you plan to use. This ensures that they are clean and free from any impurities. Next, peel and chop the vegetables as required by your recipe. The size of the chop depends on your preference and the program you intend to use. For chunky soups, you can leave the pieces larger, while smooth soups require smaller, uniform cuts.

Prepare Proteins and Additional Ingredients

If your soup recipe calls for proteins like chicken, beef, or seafood, prepare them by cutting them into appropriately sized pieces. Additionally, gather any extra ingredients such as herbs, spices, or aromatics that will enhance the flavour of your soup. Having everything ready before you start the soup maker ensures a smooth cooking process.

Add Ingredients to the Soup Maker

With your ingredients prepped and ready, it's time to assemble them in the soup maker. Follow these steps to ensure everything is in place:

Blending Jug Placement

Open the lid of your soup maker and locate the blending jug or container. It's essential to check that the blending jug is clean and free from any residue from previous uses.

Ingredient Placement

Carefully place your prepared ingredients into the blending jug. It's essential not to exceed the maximum fill line indicated on the jug. Overfilling can lead to spillage and affect the blending process. Ensure that you distribute the ingredients evenly in the jug.

Select the Desired Program

One of the key conveniences of a soup maker is the availability of preset programs tailored to different types of soups. These programs are designed to simplify the cooking process and eliminate guesswork. Here's how to choose the right program:

Program Selection

On the control panel of your soup maker, you'll find buttons or a digital display with program options. Depending on your model, you may have choices such as „smooth," „chunky," „puree," and more. Select the program that aligns with the type of soup you're preparing. For instance, if you're making a creamy tomato soup, choose the „smooth" program.

Start the Soup Maker

Once you've selected the appropriate program, it's time to initiate the cooking process. Here's how to get your soup maker up and running:

Start Button

Locate the start button on your soup maker's control panel. In most cases, it will be clearly marked as „start" or „on." Press this button to commence the blending and heating process.

Wait for Completion

Your soup maker is now in control of the cooking process, and you can sit back and relax. The time it takes for your soup to be ready varies depending on the model and the selected program. Typically, you can expect your soup to be prepared within 20-30 minutes.

During this time, your soup maker will heat the ingredients, blend them to your desired consistency, and maintain the temperature until it reaches the perfect serving temperature. Some models also have a timer display, allowing you to monitor the progress.

Serve and Enjoy

When the soup maker has completed its cycle, it will signal that your homemade soup is ready. Here's how to complete the process and savour the fruits of your labour:

Safely Remove the Blending Jug

Carefully open the lid of your soup maker and use oven mitts or a kitchen towel to handle the hot blending jug. Avoid direct contact with the hot surface.

Serve Your Delicious Homemade Soup

With the blending jug in hand, carefully pour your piping hot soup into serving bowls or cups. Take a moment to appreciate the aroma and the beautiful texture of your homemade creation.

Season and Garnish

Before serving, you have the opportunity to season your soup to taste. Add salt, pepper, herbs, or spices as needed. You can also garnish your soup with fresh herbs, a drizzle of olive oil, a dollop of sour cream, or a sprinkle of grated cheese to elevate the flavours and presentation.

Now, you're ready to enjoy your delightful homemade soup. Whether you're serving it as a comforting meal on a chilly evening or as a starter at a dinner party, the satisfaction of creating a delicious soup with your soup maker is truly rewarding.

In conclusion, using a soup maker is a straightforward and efficient process that simplifies homemade soup preparation. By following these basic operating instructions, you can maximise the benefits of your soup maker and explore a world of culinary possibilities. So, roll up your sleeves, gather your ingredients, and let your soup maker do the work while you savour the delightful results.

CHAPTER 4:
SOUP MAKING 101

Creating soups with a soup maker is a breeze, but there are a few essential steps to follow to ensure that your soups turn out perfectly every time.

4.1 PREPARING INGREDIENTS

The key to a great soup is using fresh, high-quality ingredients. Here are some general guidelines for preparing ingredients:

- **Vegetables**: Wash, peel (if necessary), and chop vegetables into evenly sized pieces. This helps ensure even cooking.
- **Proteins**: If you're using meat or poultry, cut it into small cubes or slices. For beans or lentils, rinse them thoroughly.
- **Herbs and Spices**: Chop fresh herbs finely, and use dried herbs and spices according to your recipe's instructions.
- **Liquid Base**: Measure out your liquid base, which can be water, vegetable broth, chicken broth, or any other preferred base.

4.2 LIQUID BASE SELECTION

Your choice of liquid base can significantly impact the flavour and texture of your soup. Here are some options:

- **Water**: Pure water can be used, but it may result in a less flavorful soup. Consider using vegetable or chicken broth for added depth.
- **Vegetable Broth**: Vegetable broth is a versatile and flavorful option for vegetarian and vegan soups.
- **Chicken Broth**: Chicken broth adds a rich and savoury flavour to your soups and pairs well with chicken or meat-based recipes.
- **Coconut Milk**: For a creamy and exotic twist, coconut milk can be used as a base for certain soups, especially those with a hint of spice.

4.3 SEASONING AND SPICES

Don't underestimate the power of seasoning and spices in your soup-making journey. Here are some essential tips:

- **Salt and Pepper:** Season your soup with salt and pepper to taste. Start with a small amount and adjust as needed throughout the cooking process.

- **Herbs and Spices**: Fresh herbs like basil, thyme, and rosemary can elevate the flavour of your soups. Spices like paprika, cumin, and turmeric add depth and complexity.
- **Acidic Ingredients**: **Ingredients** like tomatoes, vinegar, or citrus juice can add a refreshing acidity to balance the flavours.
- **Sweeteners**: A touch of sweetness from honey, sugar, or maple syrup can enhance the overall taste profile, especially in certain vegetable-based soups.

4.4 TIMING AND TEMPERATURE

Different ingredients require different cooking times and temperatures. Here are some general guidelines:

- **Root Vegetables**: Harder vegetables like carrots, potatoes, and beetroots may need more time to soften. Start by cooking these before adding softener ingredients.
- **Leafy Greens:** Delicate ingredients like spinach or kale should be added towards the end of the cooking process to preserve their vibrant colour and nutrients.
- **Proteins**: If you're using proteins like chicken, beef, or seafood, it's essential to ensure they're fully cooked before serving.
- **Spices**: Be cautious with potent spices like chilli powder or cayenne. Add them gradually and taste as you go to avoid overpowering your soup.

CHAPTER 5:
WHAT KIND OF INGREDIENTS WORK WELL IN A SOUP MAKER?

When using a soup maker, there are various ingredients that work well to create delicious and satisfying soups. Here are some common ingredients that you can use in your soup maker:

1. **Vegetables:** Vegetables are a staple in most soups. Common choices include onions, garlic, carrots, celery, bell peppers, tomatoes, potatoes, and leeks. You can use fresh or frozen vegetables, making it convenient to whip up a batch of soup.

2. **Broth or Stock:** To enhance the flavour of your soup, you can use vegetable broth, chicken broth, beef broth, or any other type of stock that complements your ingredients. You can use store-bought or homemade broth for a richer flavour.

3. **Protein:** Depending on your dietary preferences, you can add protein sources like chicken, beef, turkey, or tofu. Ensure the protein is cut into small pieces to cook evenly in the soup maker.

4. **Legumes:** Beans, lentils, and chickpeas are excellent additions to soups. They add protein, fibre, and a hearty texture to your soup. Pre-soak dried legumes or use canned ones for convenience.

5. **Grains:** Rice, pasta, barley, or quinoa can be used to add substance and thickness to your soup. Adjust the cooking time and add them during the appropriate stage to ensure they cook properly.

6. **Herbs and Spices:** Fresh herbs like basil, thyme, parsley, and dried spices such as cumin, paprika, oregano, and bay leaves can infuse your soup with flavour. Be mindful of the quantity, as spices can quickly overpower the taste.

7. **Dairy or Dairy Alternatives:** Cream, milk, or non-dairy alternatives like coconut milk or almond milk can be used to make creamy soups. Add these towards the end of the cooking process to prevent curdling.

8. **Seafood:** If you enjoy seafood, consider adding shrimp, fish, or mussels to your soup. Seafood cooks quickly, so add it towards the end of the cooking cycle to prevent overcooking.

9. **Noodles:** For noodle-based soups, such as chicken noodle or ramen, add noodles towards the end of the cooking cycle, as they only require a short cooking time.

10. **Garnishes:** Fresh garnishes like chopped spring onions, coriander, grated cheese, or a dollop of sour cream can add a burst of freshness and texture to your finished soup.

Remember that the order in which you add ingredients and the cooking times may vary depending on your specific soup maker model. Always refer to the manufacturer's instructions for guidance on how to use your particular machine effectively.

Experiment with different combinations of these ingredients to create your own unique and flavourful soups in your soup maker. Don't be afraid to get creative and adjust seasonings to suit your taste preferences.

CHAPTER 6:
TIPS AND TRICKS FOR SOUP MAKER SUCCESS

Now that you're well-acquainted with the basics of soup making, let's dive into some tips and tricks to elevate your soup maker game.

6.1 MAXIMISING FLAVOUR

6.1.1 Sautéing Ingredients
If your soup maker has a sauté function, use it to sauté onions, garlic, and other aromatic ingredients before adding the liquid base. This step enhances the depth of flavour in your soup.

6.1.2 Toasting Spices
Toasting spices like cumin seeds or coriander seeds in a dry, hot pan for a minute or two can intensify their flavours. Add them to your soup maker for a delightful aroma.

6.1.3 Browning Proteins
When using meats or proteins, consider browning them in a separate pan before adding them to the soup maker. This can add a savoury dimension to your soup.

6.2 THICKENING AND TEXTURE ENHANCEMENT

6.2.1 Using Potatoes or Beans
For a creamy texture without heavy cream, add cooked and blended potatoes or white beans to your soup. They act as natural thickeners.

6.2.2 Incorporating Coconut Milk
Coconut milk not only adds creaminess but also imparts a pleasant, exotic flavour to your soups. Use it sparingly for a hint of richness.

6.2.3 Adjusting Liquid Levels
You can control the thickness of your soup by adjusting the liquid levels. If it's too thick, add more liquid, and if it's too thin, let it cook longer or add less liquid initially.

6.3 STORING AND REHEATING SOUP

6.3.1 Freezing Soup
Soup makers allow you to make large batches of soup. To avoid waste, freeze leftover soup in portion-sized containers for future meals.

6.3.2 Reheating
When reheating soup, use a saucepan or microwave rather than the soup maker. High temperatures can damage the blending and heating elements if there's no liquid.

6.4 SOUP MAKER MAINTENANCE

6.4.1 Regular Cleaning
After each use, clean your soup maker thoroughly according to the manufacturer's instructions. This prevents the buildup of residue and ensures a longer lifespan.

6.4.2 Descaling
If you have hard water, consider descaling your soup maker periodically to remove mineral deposits. Follow the manufacturer's recommendations for descaling solutions.

6.4.3 Blade Maintenance
Inspect the blender blades regularly for any signs of wear or damage. Replace them if necessary to maintain optimal blending performance.

With these tips and tricks, you'll be able to create soups that are not only delicious but also impressively flavorful and textured.

Now, let's move on to Chapter 7, where we'll address common issues you might encounter with your soup maker.

CHAPTER 7:
TROUBLESHOOTING COMMON SOUP MAKER ISSUES

Soup makers are reliable kitchen appliances, but like any gadget, they can sometimes run into problems. Here are solutions to some common issues you might encounter:

7.1 SOUP TOO THIN OR WATERY

- **Issue**: Your soup has turned out thinner than expected.

Solution:

- Add thickening agents like cooked and blended potatoes or white beans.
- Simmer your soup without the lid for a longer duration to allow excess moisture to evaporate.

7.2 SOUP TOO THICK OR OVERCOOKED

- **Issue**: Your soup is overly thick or overcooked.

Solution:

- Gradually add more liquid and re-blend until the desired consistency is achieved.
- Dilute the soup with additional broth or water if necessary.

7.3 UNUSUAL NOISES OR MALFUNCTIONS

- **Issue**: Your soup maker is making strange noises or not functioning correctly.

Solution:

- Turn off and unplug the appliance immediately if you notice unusual noises or malfunctions.
- Consult the manufacturer's manual for guidance on addressing specific issues.
- If the problem persists, contact customer support for professional assistance or repairs.

In most cases, these troubleshooting steps should help you overcome minor issues with your soup maker.

However, if you encounter persistent problems, it's best to seek assistance from the manufacturer or a qualified technician.

CHAPTER 8:
FREQUENTLY ASKED QUESTIONS (FAQS)

In this chapter, we'll address some common questions and concerns that soup maker users often have.

8.1 CAN I MAKE MORE THAN SOUP?

Absolutely! While soup makers are designed primarily for soups, many models have additional functions that allow you to make a variety of dishes.

You can use them to prepare smoothies, sauces, purees, and even steam vegetables.

8.2 ARE SOUP MAKERS SAFE TO USE?

Yes, soup makers are generally safe to use when used according to the manufacturer's instructions.

However, it's crucial to follow safety guidelines, such as keeping the lid securely in place during operation, to prevent accidents.

8.3 HOW DO I CLEAN MY SOUP MAKER?

Cleaning your soup maker is simple. Most models have removable and dishwasher-safe parts, making cleanup a breeze.

Be sure to unplug the appliance before cleaning and follow the manufacturer's cleaning instructions.

8.4 CAN I MAKE SMOOTHIES IN A SOUP MAKER?

Some soup makers have a smoothie function, making it possible to prepare smoothies with ease. However, it's essential to check your specific model's capabilities and guidelines to ensure safe and effective smoothie preparation.

CHAPTER 9:
RECAP

By now, you should be well-versed in what soup makers are, how to choose the perfect one, and how to create delicious soups and more.

9.1 RECAP AND KEY TAKEAWAYS

- Soup makers are versatile kitchen appliances that simplify soup preparation.
- When choosing a soup maker, consider factors like size, power, blade quality, and additional features.
- Proper setup and safety precautions are essential before using your soup maker.
- Preparing ingredients, selecting the right liquid base, and seasoning effectively are key to crafting delicious soups.
- Don't forget to explore various soup recipes and get creative with your soup maker.
- Enhance your soup-making skills with tips for maximising flavour, texture, and proper maintenance.
- Troubleshoot common soup maker issues to ensure smooth operation.
- Consult FAQs to address any lingering questions about your soup maker.

EXCLUSIVE BONUS

40 Weight Loss Recipes

&

14 Days Meal Plan

Scan the QR-Code and receive
the FREE download:

CLASSIC SOUP MAKER RECIPES

Soups have always been the cornerstone of comfort food. Simple ingredients, when simmered together, transform into a medley of flavours that warm the soul and satisfy the stomach. Whether it's the robust thickness of a creamy chowder or the delicate clarity of a consommé, the versatility of soups has been celebrated for generations.

In this chapter, we dive deep into the world of classic soups. These are the recipes that have stood the test of time, beloved by families for their reliable taste and the fond memories they invoke. Using a soup maker streamlines the process, making it easier for everyone to recreate these timeless dishes at home.

From velvety tomato soup paired with a golden toasted cheese sandwich to the hearty embrace of a traditional vegetable broth, classic soups are a testament to the magic that happens when simple ingredients are combined with love and patience. Let's embark on this culinary exploration, revisiting the classics and perhaps introducing you to a few you've yet to try.

1. CREAMY TOMATO BASIL SOUP

This classic tomato soup is elevated with the addition of fresh basil and a creamy texture.

Nutritional Information (per serving):
Calories: 180 kcal | Carbohydrates: 25g | Protein: 4g | Fat: 8g

INGREDIENTS:

- 500g ripe tomatoes, halved
- 1 onion, chopped
- 2 cloves garlic, minced
- 250ml fresh basil leaves
- 400ml vegetable broth
- 200ml heavy cream
- Salt and pepper to taste

INSTRUCTIONS:

1 Place tomatoes, onion, and garlic in the soup maker.
2 Add vegetable broth and basil leaves.
3 Set the soup maker to the "smooth" setting and let it blend and cook.
4 Once done, add heavy cream, salt, and pepper. Blend again until smooth.
5 Serve hot.

2. BUTTERNUT SQUASH SOUP

A comforting and nutritious soup featuring the sweetness of butternut squash.

Nutritional Information (per serving):
Calories: 150 kcal | Carbohydrates: 30g | Protein: 3g | Fat: 2g

INGREDIENTS:

- 600g butternut squash, peeled and diced
- 1 onion, chopped
- 2 carrots, chopped
- 2 cloves garlic, minced
- 1 tsp ground cumin
- 1 litre vegetable broth
- Salt and pepper to taste

INSTRUCTIONS:

1 Place butternut squash, onion, carrots, and garlic in the soup maker.
2 Add vegetable broth and ground cumin.
3 Set the soup maker to the "smooth" setting and let it blend and cook.
4 Season with salt and pepper to taste.
5 Serve hot.

3. LEEK AND POTATO SOUP

A classic British soup that's creamy, hearty, and perfect for a chilly day.

Nutritional Information (per serving):
Calories: 220 kcal | Carbohydrates: 40g | Protein: 4g | Fat: 6g

INGREDIENTS:

- 400g potatoes, peeled and diced
- 2 leeks, sliced
- 1 onion, chopped
- 1 litre vegetable broth
- 200ml milk (or a dairy-free alternative)
- Salt and pepper to taste

INSTRUCTIONS:

1 Place potatoes, leeks, and onion in the soup maker.

2 Add vegetable broth and milk.

3 Set the soup maker to the "smooth" setting and let it blend and cook.

4 Season with salt and pepper to taste.

5 Serve hot with a sprinkle of chopped fresh chives, if desired.

4. LENTIL AND SPINACH SOUP

A nutritious and protein-packed soup featuring lentils and fresh spinach.

Nutritional Information (per serving):
Calories: 220 kcal | Carbohydrates: 35g | Protein: 12g | Fat: 2g

INGREDIENTS:

- 200g red lentils
- 1 onion, chopped
- 2 carrots, chopped
- 2 cloves garlic, minced
- 150g fresh spinach
- 1 litre vegetable broth
- 1 tsp cumin
- Salt and pepper to taste

INSTRUCTIONS:

1 Place red lentils, onion, carrots, and garlic in the soup maker.

2 Add vegetable broth and cumin.

3 Set the soup maker to the "smooth" setting and let it blend and cook.

4 Stir in fresh spinach until wilted.

5 Season with salt and pepper to taste.

6 Serve hot.

5. MUSHROOM AND BARLEY SOUP

A hearty and earthy soup with the goodness of mushrooms and barley.

Nutritional Information (per serving):
Calories: 250 kcal | Carbohydrates: 45g | Protein: 8g | Fat: 5g

INGREDIENTS:
- 250g mushrooms, sliced
- 1 onion, chopped
- 2 cloves garlic, minced
- 100g pearl barley
- 1 litre vegetable broth
- 1 tsp thyme
- Salt and pepper to taste

INSTRUCTIONS:
1 Place mushrooms, onion, and garlic in the soup maker.
2 Add vegetable broth, pearl barley, and thyme.
3 Set the soup maker to the "smooth" setting and let it blend and cook.
4 Season with salt and pepper to taste.
5 Serve hot.

6. BROCCOLI AND CHEDDAR SOUP

A creamy and cheesy soup with the goodness of broccoli.

Nutritional Information (per serving):
Calories: 280 kcal | Carbohydrates: 20g | Protein: 10g | Fat: 18g

INGREDIENTS:
- 500g broccoli florets
- 1 onion, chopped
- 2 cloves garlic, minced
- 400ml vegetable broth
- 200ml milk (or a dairy-free alternative)
- 150g grated cheddar cheese
- Salt and pepper to taste

INSTRUCTIONS:
1 Place broccoli, onion, and garlic in the soup maker.
2 Add vegetable broth and milk.
3 Set the soup maker to the "smooth" setting and let it blend and cook.
4 Stir in grated cheddar cheese until melted and smooth.
5 Season with salt and pepper to taste.
6 Serve hot.

7. SWEET POTATO AND COCONUT SOUP

A rich and creamy soup with the natural sweetness of sweet potatoes and the tropical flavour of coconut milk.

Nutritional Information (per serving):
Calories: 220 kcal | Carbohydrates: 30g | Protein: 3g | Fat: 11g

INGREDIENTS:
- 500g sweet potatoes, peeled and diced
- 1 onion, chopped
- 2 cloves garlic, minced
- 400ml coconut milk
- 400ml vegetable broth
- 1 tsp curry powder
- Salt and pepper to taste

INSTRUCTIONS:
1 Place sweet potatoes, onion, and garlic in the soup maker.
2 Add coconut milk, vegetable broth, and curry powder.
3 Set the soup maker to the "smooth" setting and let it blend and cook.
4 Season with salt and pepper to taste.
5 Serve hot.

8. SPINACH AND POTATO SOUP

A light and nutritious soup with the earthy flavours of spinach and potatoes.

Nutritional Information (per serving):
Calories: 180 kcal | Carbohydrates: 30g | Protein: 6g | Fat: 4g

INGREDIENTS:
- 400g potatoes, peeled and diced
- 200g fresh spinach
- 1 onion, chopped
- 2 cloves garlic, minced
- 1 litre vegetable broth
- Salt and pepper to taste

INSTRUCTIONS:
1 Place potatoes, spinach, onion, and garlic in the soup maker.
2 Add vegetable broth.
3 Set the soup maker to the "smooth" setting and let it blend and cook.
4 Season with salt and pepper to taste.
5 Serve hot with a drizzle of olive oil, if desired.

9. RED PEPPER AND LENTIL SOUP

A vibrant and hearty soup with the sweetness of red peppers and the protein punch of lentils.

Nutritional Information (per serving):
Calories: 240 kcal | Carbohydrates: 40g | Protein: 9g | Fat: 5g

INGREDIENTS:

- 3 red bell peppers, diced
- 200g red lentils
- 1 onion, chopped
- 2 cloves garlic, minced
- 1 litre vegetable broth
- 1 tsp smoked paprika
- Salt and pepper to taste

INSTRUCTIONS:

1 Place red peppers, lentils, onion, and garlic in the soup maker.
2 Add vegetable broth and smoked paprika.
3 Set the soup maker to the "smooth" setting and let it blend and cook.
4 Season with salt and pepper to taste.
5 Serve hot.

10. SPINACH AND WHITE BEAN SOUP

A wholesome soup featuring creamy white beans and nutritious spinach.

Nutritional Information (per serving):
Calories: 220 kcal | Carbohydrates: 35g | Protein: 9g | Fat: 4g

INGREDIENTS:

- 400g white beans (cannellini or navy), cooked or canned
- 200g fresh spinach
- 1 onion, chopped
- 2 cloves garlic, minced
- 1 litre vegetable broth
- 1 tsp Italian seasoning
- Salt and pepper to taste

INSTRUCTIONS:

1 Place white beans, spinach, onion, and garlic in the soup maker.
2 Add vegetable broth and Italian seasoning.
3 Set the soup maker to the "smooth" setting and let it blend and cook.
4 Season with salt and pepper to taste.
5 Serve hot with a sprinkle of grated Parmesan cheese, if desired.

11. ROASTED RED PEPPER AND TOMATO SOUP

A smoky and flavorful soup with the sweetness of roasted red peppers and the tanginess of tomatoes.

Nutritional Information (per serving):
Calories: 150 kcal | Carbohydrates: 20g | Protein: 3g | Fat: 7g

INGREDIENTS:
- 3 red bell peppers, roasted and peeled
- 400g canned tomatoes
- 1 onion, chopped
- 2 cloves garlic, minced
- 1 litre vegetable broth
- 1 tsp smoked paprika
- Salt and pepper to taste

INSTRUCTIONS:
1 Place roasted red peppers, canned tomatoes, onion, and garlic in the soup maker.

2 Add vegetable broth and smoked paprika.

3 Set the soup maker to the "smooth" setting and let it blend and cook.

4 Season with salt and pepper to taste.

5 Serve hot.

12. CARROT AND GINGER SOUP

A vibrant and spicy soup with the earthy sweetness of carrots and a hint of ginger.

Nutritional Information (per serving):
Calories: 180 kcal | Carbohydrates: 30g | Protein: 4g | Fat: 5g

INGREDIENTS:
- 500g carrots, peeled and chopped
- 1 onion, chopped
- 2 cloves garlic, minced
- 1 thumb-sized piece of ginger, peeled and minced
- 1 litre vegetable broth
- 200ml coconut milk
- Salt and pepper to taste

INSTRUCTIONS:
1 Place carrots, onion, garlic, and ginger in the soup maker.

2 Add vegetable broth and coconut milk.

3 Set the soup maker to the "smooth" setting and let it blend and cook.

4 Season with salt and pepper to taste.

5 Serve hot.

13. MUSHROOM AND WILD RICE SOUP

A hearty and earthy soup featuring mushrooms and nutty wild rice.

Nutritional Information (per serving):
Calories: 250 kcal | Carbohydrates: 35g | Protein: 7g | Fat: 9g

INGREDIENTS:

- 250g mushrooms, sliced
- 100g wild rice, cooked
- 1 onion, chopped
- 2 cloves garlic, minced
- 1 litre vegetable broth
- 200ml heavy cream (or a dairy-free alternative)
- Salt and pepper to taste

INSTRUCTIONS:

1 Place mushrooms, cooked wild rice, onion, and garlic in the soup maker.
2 Add vegetable broth and heavy cream.
3 Set the soup maker to the "smooth" setting and let it blend and cook.
4 Season with salt and pepper to taste.
5 Serve hot.

14. THAI COCONUT NOODLE SOUP

A fragrant and creamy Thai-inspired soup with coconut milk, tofu, and rice noodles.

Nutritional Information (per serving):
Calories: 300 kcal | Carbohydrates: 35g | Protein: 10g | Fat: 14g

INGREDIENTS:

- 200g rice noodles, cooked
- 200g tofu, cubed
- 400ml coconut milk
- 1 litre vegetable broth
- 1 red bell pepper, sliced
- 1 thumb-sized piece of ginger, peeled and minced
- 2 cloves garlic, minced
- 1 tbsp red curry paste
- Salt and pepper to taste

INSTRUCTIONS:

1 Place cooked rice noodles, tofu, red bell pepper, ginger, garlic, and red curry paste in the soup maker.
2 Add coconut milk and vegetable broth.
3 Set the soup maker to the "smooth" setting and let it blend and cook.
4 Season with salt and pepper to taste.
5 Serve hot, garnished with fresh coriander and lime wedges.

15. POTATO AND LEEK SOUP

A comforting and creamy soup featuring the classic combination of potatoes and leeks.

Nutritional Information (per serving):
Calories: 220 kcal | Carbohydrates: 40g | Protein: 5g | Fat: 5g

INGREDIENTS:

- 500g potatoes, peeled and diced
- 2 leeks, sliced
- 1 onion, chopped
- 2 cloves garlic, minced
- 1 litre vegetable broth
- 150ml heavy cream (or a dairy-free alternative)
- Salt and pepper to taste

INSTRUCTIONS:

1 Place potatoes, leeks, onion, and garlic in the soup maker.
2 Add vegetable broth and heavy cream.
3 Set the soup maker to the "smooth" setting and let it blend and cook.
4 Season with salt and pepper to taste.
5 Serve hot with a drizzle of olive oil, if desired.

16. SPINACH AND MUSHROOM BARLEY SOUP

A hearty and wholesome soup with the goodness of spinach, mushrooms, and barley.

Nutritional Information (per serving):
Calories: 240 kcal | Carbohydrates: 35g | Protein: 8g | Fat: 5g

INGREDIENTS:

- 200g barley, cooked
- 200g fresh spinach
- 250g mushrooms, sliced
- 1 onion, chopped
- 2 cloves garlic, minced
- 1 litre vegetable broth
- 1 tsp thyme
- Salt and pepper to taste

INSTRUCTIONS:

1 Place cooked barley, fresh spinach, mushrooms, onion, and garlic in the soup maker.
2 Add vegetable broth and thyme.
3 Set the soup maker to the "smooth" setting and let it blend and cook.
4 Season with salt and pepper to taste.
5 Serve hot.

17. SPINACH AND LENTIL SOUP

A nutritious and protein-packed soup featuring spinach and red lentils.

Nutritional Information (per serving):
Calories: 220 kcal | Carbohydrates: 30g | Protein: 10g | Fat: 4g

INGREDIENTS:

- 200g red lentils
- 200g fresh spinach
- 1 onion, chopped
- 2 cloves garlic, minced
- 1 litre vegetable broth
- 1 tsp cumin
- Salt and pepper to taste

INSTRUCTIONS:

1. Place red lentils, fresh spinach, onion, and garlic in the soup maker.
2. Add vegetable broth and cumin.
3. Set the soup maker to the "smooth" setting and let it blend and cook.
4. Season with salt and pepper to taste.
5. Serve hot.

18. TOMATO AND QUINOA SOUP

A protein-rich and flavorful soup featuring quinoa and ripe tomatoes.

Nutritional Information (per serving):
Calories: 250 kcal | Carbohydrates: 40g | Protein: 8g | Fat: 5g

INGREDIENTS:

- 200g quinoa, rinsed
- 500g ripe tomatoes, diced
- 1 onion, chopped
- 2 cloves garlic, minced
- 1 litre vegetable broth
- 1 tsp Italian seasoning
- Salt and pepper to taste

INSTRUCTIONS:

1. Place quinoa, diced tomatoes, onion, and garlic in the soup maker.
2. Add vegetable broth and Italian seasoning.
3. Set the soup maker to the "smooth" setting and let it blend and cook.
4. Season with salt and pepper to taste.
5. Serve hot.

19. CAULIFLOWER AND BROCCOLI SOUP

A creamy and nutritious soup featuring cauliflower and broccoli.

Nutritional Information (per serving):
Calories: 180 kcal | Carbohydrates: 25g | Protein: 7g | Fat: 7g

INGREDIENTS:

- 500g cauliflower florets
- 500g broccoli florets
- 1 onion, chopped
- 2 cloves garlic, minced
- 1 litre vegetable broth
- 200ml heavy cream (or a dairy-free alternative)
- Salt and pepper to taste

INSTRUCTIONS:

1 Place cauliflower, broccoli, onion, and garlic in the soup maker.

2 Add vegetable broth and heavy cream.

3 Set the soup maker to the "smooth" setting and let it blend and cook.

4 Season with salt and pepper to taste.

5 Serve hot.

20. SPICY BLACK BEAN SOUP

A zesty and satisfying soup featuring black beans, tomatoes, and spices.

Nutritional Information (per serving):
Calories: 220 kcal | Carbohydrates: 40g | Protein: 10g | Fat: 2g

INGREDIENTS:

- 400g canned black beans, drained and rinsed
- 400g canned diced tomatoes
- 1 onion, chopped
- 2 cloves garlic, minced
- 1 tsp chilli powder
- 1 litre vegetable broth
- Salt and pepper to taste

INSTRUCTIONS:

1 Place black beans, diced tomatoes, onion, and garlic in the soup maker.

2 Add vegetable broth and chilli powder.

3 Set the soup maker to the "smooth" setting and let it blend and cook.

4 Season with salt and pepper to taste.

5 Serve hot, garnished with chopped fresh coriander and a dollop of yoghurt (or dairy-free yoghurts).

21. SPINACH AND CHICKPEA SOUP

A nutritious and hearty soup featuring chickpeas and fresh spinach.

Nutritional Information (per serving):
Calories: 250 kcal | Carbohydrates: 40g | Protein: 10g | Fat: 5g

INGREDIENTS:

- 400g canned chickpeas, drained and rinsed
- 200g fresh spinach
- 1 onion, chopped
- 2 cloves garlic, minced
- 1 litre vegetable broth
- 1 tsp cumin
- Salt and pepper to taste

INSTRUCTIONS:

1. Place chickpeas, fresh spinach, onion, and garlic in the soup maker.
2. Add vegetable broth and cumin.
3. Set the soup maker to the "smooth" setting and let it blend and cook.
4. Season with salt and pepper to taste.
5. Serve hot.

22. SWEET CORN AND POTATO CHOWDER

A creamy and comforting chowder featuring sweet corn and tender potatoes.

Nutritional Information (per serving):
Calories: 220 kcal | Carbohydrates: 40g | Protein: 6g | Fat: 5g

INGREDIENTS:

- 400g sweet corn kernels (frozen or canned)
- 500g potatoes, peeled and diced
- 1 onion, chopped
- 2 cloves garlic, minced
- 1 litre vegetable broth
- 200ml milk (or a dairy-free alternative)
- Salt and pepper to taste

INSTRUCTIONS:

1. Place sweet corn kernels, diced potatoes, onion, and garlic in the soup maker.
2. Add vegetable broth and milk.
3. Set the soup maker to the "smooth" setting and let it blend and cook.
4. Season with salt and pepper to taste.
5. Serve hot.

23. COURGETTE AND BASIL SOUP

A light and refreshing soup with the summery flavours of courgette and fresh basil.

Nutritional Information (per serving):
Calories: 160 kcal | Carbohydrates: 20g | Protein: 4g | Fat: 8g

INGREDIENTS:
- 500g courgette, sliced
- 1 onion, chopped
- 2 cloves garlic, minced
- 1 litre vegetable broth
- 250ml fresh basil leaves
- 2 tbsp olive oil
- Salt and pepper to taste

INSTRUCTIONS:
1 Place courgette, onion, and garlic in the soup maker.
2 Add vegetable broth and olive oil.
3 Set the soup maker to the "smooth" setting and let it blend and cook.
4 Add fresh basil leaves and blend again until smooth.
5 Season with salt and pepper to taste.
6 Serve hot.

24. MOROCCAN LENTIL SOUP

A flavorful and aromatic soup with red lentils and Moroccan spices.

Nutritional Information (per serving):
Calories: 230 kcal | Carbohydrates: 30g | Protein: 10g | Fat: 7g

INGREDIENTS:
- 200g red lentils
- 1 onion, chopped
- 2 cloves garlic, minced
- 1 carrot, chopped
- 1 tsp ground cumin
- 1 tsp ground coriander
- 1 tsp paprika
- 1 litre vegetable broth
- Salt and pepper to taste

INSTRUCTIONS:
1 Place red lentils, onion, garlic, carrot, and spices in the soup maker.
2 Add vegetable broth.
3 Set the soup maker to the "smooth" setting and let it blend and cook.
4 Season with salt and pepper to taste.
5 Serve hot, garnished with a dollop of yoghurt (or dairy-free yoghurts) and chopped fresh coriander.

25. CREAMY MUSHROOM AND WILD RICE SOUP

A rich and indulgent soup featuring mushrooms, wild rice, and creamy coconut milk.

Nutritional Information (per serving):
Calories: 280 kcal | Carbohydrates: 35g | Protein: 8g | Fat: 14g

INGREDIENTS:
- 250g mushrooms, sliced
- 100g wild rice, cooked
- 1 onion, chopped
- 2 cloves garlic, minced
- 400ml coconut milk
- 1 litre vegetable broth
- Salt and pepper to taste

INSTRUCTIONS:
1 Place mushrooms, cooked wild rice, onion, and garlic in the soup maker.
2 Add coconut milk and vegetable broth.
3 Set the soup maker to the "smooth" setting and let it blend and cook.
4 Season with salt and pepper to taste.
5 Serve hot.

26. SPINACH AND TOMATO ORZO SOUP

A comforting and satisfying soup featuring orzo pasta, spinach, and diced tomatoes.

Nutritional Information (per serving):
Calories: 220 kcal | Carbohydrates: 40g | Protein: 8g | Fat: 3g

INGREDIENTS:
- 200g orzo pasta
- 200g fresh spinach
- 400g canned diced tomatoes
- 1 onion, chopped
- 2 cloves garlic, minced
- 1 litre vegetable broth
- Salt and pepper to taste

INSTRUCTIONS:
1 Place orzo pasta, fresh spinach, diced tomatoes, onion, and garlic in the soup maker.
2 Add vegetable broth.
3 Set the soup maker to the "smooth" setting and let it blend and cook.
4 Season with salt and pepper to taste.
5 Serve hot.

27. SPICY SWEET POTATO SOUP

A bold and spicy soup with the natural sweetness of sweet potatoes.

Nutritional Information (per serving):
Calories: 220 kcal | Carbohydrates: 40g | Protein: 4g | Fat: 5g

INGREDIENTS:

- 500g sweet potatoes, peeled and diced
- 1 onion, chopped
- 2 cloves garlic, minced
- 1 thumb-sized piece of ginger, peeled and minced
- 1 tsp curry powder
- 1 litre vegetable broth
- 200ml coconut milk
- Salt and pepper to taste

INSTRUCTIONS:

1 Place sweet potatoes, onion, garlic, ginger, and curry powder in the soup maker.

2 Add vegetable broth and coconut milk.

3 Set the soup maker to the "smooth" setting and let it blend and cook.

4 Season with salt and pepper to taste.

5 Serve hot.

28. SPINACH AND RED LENTIL SOUP

A nutritious and protein-packed soup featuring red lentils and fresh spinach.

Nutritional Information (per serving):
Calories: 230 kcal | Carbohydrates: 35g | Protein: 10g | Fat: 3g

INGREDIENTS:

- 200g red lentils
- 200g fresh spinach
- 1 onion, chopped
- 2 cloves garlic, minced
- 1 litre vegetable broth
- 1 tsp cumin
- Salt and pepper to taste

INSTRUCTIONS:

1 Place red lentils, fresh spinach, onion, and garlic in the soup maker.

2 Add vegetable broth and cumin.

3 Set the soup maker to the "smooth" setting and let it blend and cook.

4 Season with salt and pepper to taste.

5 Serve hot.

29. CREAMY ASPARAGUS SOUP

A delicate and creamy soup with the seasonal flavour of asparagus.

Nutritional Information (per serving):
Calories: 180 kcal | Carbohydrates: 20g | Protein: 6g | Fat: 10g

INGREDIENTS:

- 500g asparagus, trimmed and chopped
- 1 onion, chopped
- 2 cloves garlic, minced
- 400ml vegetable broth
- 200ml heavy cream (or a dairy-free alternative)
- Salt and pepper to taste

INSTRUCTIONS:

1 Place asparagus, onion, and garlic in the soup maker.

2 Add vegetable broth and heavy cream.

3 Set the soup maker to the "smooth" setting and let it blend and cook.

4 Season with salt and pepper to taste.

5 Serve hot.

30. SPICY PUMPKIN SOUP

A warming and spicy soup with the autumnal flavour of pumpkin.

Nutritional Information (per serving):
Calories: 220 kcal | Carbohydrates: 30g | Protein: 4g | Fat: 10g

INGREDIENTS:

- 500g pumpkin, peeled and diced
- 1 onion, chopped
- 2 cloves garlic, minced
- 1 thumb-sized piece of ginger, peeled and minced
- 1 tsp curry powder
- 1 litre vegetable broth
- 200ml coconut milk
- Salt and pepper to taste

INSTRUCTIONS:

1 Place pumpkin, onion, garlic, ginger, and curry powder in the soup maker.

2 Add vegetable broth and coconut milk.

3 Set the soup maker to the "smooth" setting and let it blend and cook.

4 Season with salt and pepper to taste.

5 Serve hot.

VEGAN SOUP RECIPES

The beauty of vegan cooking lies in its emphasis on harnessing the pure, unadulterated power of plants. This is especially evident in soups, where the symphony of natural ingredients comes together to create flavours both rich and profound, without the need for animal products.

In this chapter, we delve into the delightful realm of vegan soups. These aren't just alternatives or substitutes for traditional recipes; they are culinary masterpieces in their own right. Every bowl showcases the diversity and depth that plant-based ingredients can offer.

Whether it's the creamy allure of a butternut squash soup without a touch of dairy or the spicy kick of a lentil and chilli stew, vegan soups promise a world of taste and texture. Using fresh vegetables, legumes, grains, and herbs, these recipes capture the essence of what it means to eat in harmony with the earth.

Embark with us on this green journey, and discover the incredible satisfaction that comes from a pot brimming with vegan goodness. Whether you're a seasoned vegan or just dabbling in plant-based cuisine, these soups are sure to tantalise your taste buds and warm your heart.

1. SPICY LENTIL AND VEGETABLE SOUP

A hearty and flavorful vegan soup packed with protein-rich lentils and an array of vegetables.

Nutritional Information (per serving):
Calories: 220 kcal | Carbohydrates: 35g | Protein: 10g | Fat: 3g

INGREDIENTS:

- 200g red lentils
- 1 onion, chopped
- 2 cloves garlic, minced
- 2 carrots, chopped
- 1 red bell pepper, chopped
- 1 tsp cumin
- 1 litre vegetable broth
- Salt and pepper to taste

INSTRUCTIONS:

1 Place red lentils, onion, garlic, carrots, red bell pepper, and cumin in the soup maker.
2 Add vegetable broth.
3 Set the soup maker to the "smooth" setting and let it blend and cook.
4 Season with salt and pepper to taste.
5 Serve hot.

2. CREAMY BROCCOLI AND ALMOND SOUP

A creamy and nutty vegan soup with the goodness of broccoli and almonds.

Nutritional Information (per serving):
Calories: 250 kcal | Carbohydrates: 25g | Protein: 9g | Fat: 14g

INGREDIENTS:

- 500g broccoli florets
- 1 onion, chopped
- 2 cloves garlic, minced
- 100g almonds, soaked and peeled
- 1 litre vegetable broth
- Salt and pepper to taste

INSTRUCTIONS:

1 Place broccoli florets, onion, garlic, and soaked almonds in the soup maker.
2 Add vegetable broth.
3 Set the soup maker to the "smooth" setting and let it blend and cook.
4 Season with salt and pepper to taste.
5 Serve hot.

3. MOROCCAN SPICED CHICKPEA SOUP

A fragrant and spicy vegan soup featuring chickpeas and Moroccan spices.

Nutritional Information (per serving):
Calories: 280 kcal | Carbohydrates: 40g | Protein: 10g | Fat: 9g

INGREDIENTS:

- 400g canned chickpeas, drained and rinsed
- 1 onion, chopped
- 2 cloves garlic, minced
- 1 carrot, chopped
- 1 tsp ground cumin
- 1 tsp ground coriander
- 1 tsp paprika
- 1 litre vegetable broth
- Salt and pepper to taste

INSTRUCTIONS:

1 Place chickpeas, onion, garlic, carrot, and spices in the soup maker.

2 Add vegetable broth.

3 Set the soup maker to the "smooth" setting and let it blend and cook.

4 Season with salt and pepper to taste.

5 Serve hot.

4. CREAMY TOMATO AND BASIL SOUP

A classic tomato soup made vegan with the addition of creamy coconut milk and fresh basil.

Nutritional Information (per serving):
Calories: 180 kcal | Carbohydrates: 20g | Protein: 4g | Fat: 11g

INGREDIENTS:

- 500g ripe tomatoes, halved
- 1 onion, chopped
- 2 cloves garlic, minced
- 250ml fresh basil leaves
- 400ml coconut milk
- 1 litre vegetable broth
- Salt and pepper to taste

INSTRUCTIONS:

1 Place tomatoes, onion, garlic, and basil leaves in the soup maker.

2 Add coconut milk and vegetable broth.

3 Set the soup maker to the "smooth" setting and let it blend and cook.

4 Season with salt and pepper to taste.

5 Serve hot.

5. SPICY SWEET POTATO AND PEANUT SOUP

A creamy and spicy vegan soup featuring the natural sweetness of sweet potatoes and the richness of peanut butter.

Nutritional Information (per serving):
Calories: 280 kcal | Carbohydrates: 30g | Protein: 8g | Fat: 16g

INGREDIENTS:

- 500g sweet potatoes, peeled and diced
- 1 onion, chopped
- 2 cloves garlic, minced
- 1 thumb-sized piece of ginger, peeled and minced
- 2 tbsp peanut butter
- 1 tsp curry powder
- 1 litre vegetable broth
- Salt and pepper to taste

INSTRUCTIONS:

1 Place sweet potatoes, onion, garlic, ginger, peanut butter, and curry powder in the soup maker.
2 Add vegetable broth.
3 Set the soup maker to the "smooth" setting and let it blend and cook.
4 Season with salt and pepper to taste.
5 Serve hot.

6. THAI COCONUT AND LEMONGRASS SOUP

A fragrant and coconut-infused vegan soup with the zing of lemongrass and Thai flavours.

Nutritional Information (per serving):
Calories: 300 kcal | Carbohydrates: 30g | Protein: 6g | Fat: 18g

INGREDIENTS:

- 400ml coconut milk
- 1 stalk lemongrass, cut into pieces
- 1 thumb-sized piece of ginger, peeled and sliced
- 2 cloves garlic, minced
- 1 red chilli pepper, chopped
- 250ml mixed vegetables (e.g., bell peppers, mushrooms, baby corn)
- 1 litre vegetable broth
- Salt and pepper to taste

INSTRUCTIONS:

1 Place coconut milk, lemongrass, ginger, garlic, chilli pepper, and mixed vegetables in the soup maker.

2 Add vegetable broth.

3 Set the soup maker to the "smooth" setting and let it blend and cook.

4 Season with salt and pepper to taste.

5 Serve hot, garnished with fresh coriander and a squeeze of lime juice.

7. CREAMY MUSHROOM AND TOFU SOUP

A rich and creamy vegan soup with the umami flavours of mushrooms and the protein punch of tofu.

Nutritional Information (per serving):
Calories: 220 kcal | Carbohydrates: 25g | Protein: 12g | Fat: 10g

INGREDIENTS:

- 250g mushrooms, sliced
- 200g tofu, cubed
- 1 onion, chopped
- 2 cloves garlic, minced
- 1 litre vegetable broth
- 200ml coconut milk
- Salt and pepper to taste

INSTRUCTIONS:

1 Place mushrooms, tofu, onion, and garlic in the soup maker.

2 Add vegetable broth and coconut milk.

3 Set the soup maker to the "smooth" setting and let it blend and cook.

4 Season with salt and pepper to taste.

5 Serve hot.

8. CREAMY SPINACH AND POTATO SOUP

A comforting and creamy vegan soup featuring spinach and tender potatoes.

Nutritional Information (per serving):
Calories: 220 kcal | Carbohydrates: 30g | Protein: 5g | Fat: 8g

INGREDIENTS:

- 500g potatoes, peeled and diced
- 200g fresh spinach
- 1 onion, chopped
- 2 cloves garlic, minced
- 200ml coconut milk
- 1 litre vegetable broth
- Salt and pepper to taste

INSTRUCTIONS:

1 Place potatoes, fresh spinach, onion, and garlic in the soup maker.
2 Add coconut milk and vegetable broth.
3 Set the soup maker to the "smooth" setting and let it blend and cook.
4 Season with salt and pepper to taste.
5 Serve hot.

9. ROASTED RED PEPPER AND CHICKPEA SOUP

A smoky and protein-packed vegan soup with the sweetness of roasted red peppers and chickpeas.

Nutritional Information (per serving):
Calories: 240 kcal | Carbohydrates: 35g | Protein: 10g | Fat: 7g

INGREDIENTS:

- 3 red bell peppers, roasted and peeled
- 400g canned chickpeas, drained and rinsed
- 1 onion, chopped
- 2 cloves garlic, minced
- 1 tsp smoked paprika
- 1 litre vegetable broth
- Salt and pepper to taste

INSTRUCTIONS:

1 Place roasted red peppers, chickpeas, onion, garlic, and smoked paprika in the soup maker.
2 Add vegetable broth.
3 Set the soup maker to the "smooth" setting and let it blend and cook.
4 Season with salt and pepper to taste.
5 Serve hot.

10. SPICY PUMPKIN AND COCONUT SOUP

A warming and spicy vegan soup with the autumnal flavour of pumpkin and creamy coconut milk.

Nutritional Information (per serving):
Calories: 250 kcal | Carbohydrates: 30g | Protein: 4g | Fat: 14g

INGREDIENTS:

- 500g pumpkin, peeled and diced
- 1 onion, chopped
- 2 cloves garlic, minced
- 1 thumb-sized piece of ginger, peeled and minced
- 1 tsp curry powder
- 400ml coconut milk
- 1 litre vegetable broth
- Salt and pepper to taste

INSTRUCTIONS:

1 Place pumpkin, onion, garlic, ginger, and curry powder in the soup maker.

2 Add coconut milk and vegetable broth.

3 Set the soup maker to the "smooth" setting and let it blend and cook.

4 Season with salt and pepper to taste.

5 Serve hot.

11. CREAMY CAULIFLOWER AND LEEK SOUP

A velvety and comforting vegan soup featuring cauliflower and leeks.

Nutritional Information (per serving):
Calories: 180 kcal | Carbohydrates: 25g | Protein: 5g | Fat: 8g

INGREDIENTS:

- 500g cauliflower florets
- 2 leeks, sliced
- 1 onion, chopped
- 2 cloves garlic, minced
- 200ml coconut milk
- 1 litre vegetable broth
- Salt and pepper to taste

INSTRUCTIONS:

1 Place cauliflower florets, leeks, onion, and garlic in the soup maker.

2 Add coconut milk and vegetable broth.

3 Set the soup maker to the "smooth" setting and let it blend and cook.

4 Season with salt and pepper to taste.

5 Serve hot.

12. CREAMY BUTTERNUT SQUASH SOUP

A creamy and velvety vegan soup featuring the sweetness of butternut squash.

Nutritional Information (per serving):
Calories: 230 kcal | Carbohydrates: 30g | Protein: 4g | Fat: 10g

INGREDIENTS:
- 500g butternut squash, peeled and diced
- 1 onion, chopped
- 2 cloves garlic, minced
- 1 tsp nutmeg
- 200ml coconut milk
- 1 litre vegetable broth
- Salt and pepper to taste

INSTRUCTIONS:
1 Place butternut squash, onion, garlic, and nutmeg in the soup maker.
2 Add coconut milk and vegetable broth.
3 Set the soup maker to the "smooth" setting and let it blend and cook.
4 Season with salt and pepper to taste.
5 Serve hot.

13. SMOKY BLACK BEAN AND CORN SOUP

A smoky and satisfying vegan soup with black beans and sweet corn.

Nutritional Information (per serving):
Calories: 220 kcal | Carbohydrates: 40g | Protein: 10g | Fat: 2g

INGREDIENTS:
- 400g canned black beans, drained and rinsed
- 200g sweet corn kernels (frozen or canned)
- 1 onion, chopped
- 2 cloves garlic, minced
- 1 tsp smoked paprika
- 1 litre vegetable broth
- Salt and pepper to taste

INSTRUCTIONS:
1 Place black beans, sweet corn kernels, onion, garlic, and smoked paprika in the soup maker.
2 Add vegetable broth.
3 Set the soup maker to the "smooth" setting and let it blend and cook.
4 Season with salt and pepper to taste.
5 Serve hot, garnished with fresh coriander and a squeeze of lime juice.

14. THAI-INSPIRED VEGETABLE NOODLE SOUP

A fragrant and noodle-filled vegan soup with Thai-inspired flavours.

Nutritional Information (per serving):
Calories: 250 kcal | Carbohydrates: 35g | Protein: 8g | Fat: 8g

INGREDIENTS:
- 200g rice noodles, cooked
- 1 carrot, sliced
- 1 red bell pepper, sliced
- 1 courgette, sliced
- 1 thumb-sized piece of ginger, peeled and minced
- 2 cloves garlic, minced
- 400ml coconut milk
- 1 litre vegetable broth
- 1 tsp red curry paste
- Salt and pepper to taste

INSTRUCTIONS:
1 Place cooked rice noodles, carrot, red bell pepper, courgette, ginger, garlic, and red curry paste in the soup maker.
2 Add coconut milk and vegetable broth.
3 Set the soup maker to the "smooth" setting and let it blend and cook.
4 Season with salt and pepper to taste.
5 Serve hot.

15. SPICY POTATO AND KALE SOUP

A hearty and spicy vegan soup featuring potatoes and nutrient-packed kale.

Nutritional Information (per serving):
Calories: 230 kcal | Carbohydrates: 30g | Protein: 6g | Fat: 10g

INGREDIENTS:
- 500g potatoes, peeled and diced
- 200g kale, stems removed and chopped
- 1 onion, chopped
- 2 cloves garlic, minced
- 1 tsp chilli flakes
- 200ml coconut milk
- 1 litre vegetable broth
- Salt and pepper to taste

INSTRUCTIONS:
1 Place potatoes, kale, onion, garlic, and chilli flakes in the soup maker.
2 Add coconut milk and vegetable broth.
3 Set the soup maker to the "smooth" setting and let it blend and cook.
4 Season with salt and pepper to taste.
5 Serve hot.

16. CREAMY SPINACH AND ARTICHOKE SOUP

A creamy and indulgent vegan soup with the classic flavours of spinach and artichoke.

Nutritional Information (per serving):
Calories: 220 kcal | Carbohydrates: 25g | Protein: 7g | Fat: 10g

INGREDIENTS:

- 200g fresh spinach
- 200g canned artichoke hearts, drained and chopped
- 1 onion, chopped
- 2 cloves garlic, minced
- 200ml coconut milk
- 1 litre vegetable broth
- Salt and pepper to taste

INSTRUCTIONS:

1 Place fresh spinach, chopped artichoke hearts, onion, and garlic in the soup maker.
2 Add coconut milk and vegetable broth.
3 Set the soup maker to the "smooth" setting and let it blend and cook.
4 Season with salt and pepper to taste.
5 Serve hot.

17. CLASSIC ASPARAGUS AND PEA SOUP

A delicate and creamy vegan soup with the flavours of seasonal asparagus and sweet peas.

Nutritional Information (per serving):
Calories: 180 kcal | Carbohydrates: 25g | Protein: 6g | Fat: 7g

INGREDIENTS:

- 500g asparagus, trimmed and chopped
- 200g peas (fresh or frozen)
- 1 onion, chopped
- 2 cloves garlic, minced
- 200ml coconut milk
- 1 litre vegetable broth
- Salt and pepper to taste

INSTRUCTIONS:

1 Place asparagus, peas, onion, and garlic in the soup maker.
2 Add coconut milk and vegetable broth.
3 Set the soup maker to the "smooth" setting and let it blend and cook.
4 Season with salt and pepper to taste.
5 Serve hot.

18. CREAMY MUSHROOM AND WILD RICE SOUP

A rich and indulgent vegan soup featuring mushrooms, wild rice, and creamy coconut milk.

Nutritional Information (per serving):
Calories: 280 kcal | Carbohydrates: 35g | Protein: 8g | Fat: 14g

INGREDIENTS:

- 250g mushrooms, sliced
- 100g wild rice, cooked
- 1 onion, chopped
- 2 cloves garlic, minced
- 400ml coconut milk
- 1 litre vegetable broth
- Salt and pepper to taste

INSTRUCTIONS:

1 Place mushrooms, cooked wild rice, onion, and garlic in the soup maker.

2 Add coconut milk and vegetable broth.

3 Set the soup maker to the "smooth" setting and let it blend and cook.

4 Season with salt and pepper to taste.

5 Serve hot.

19. CREAMY POTATO AND LEEK SOUP

A classic and creamy vegan soup with the comforting flavours of potatoes and leeks.

Nutritional Information (per serving):
Calories: 200 kcal | Carbohydrates: 30g | Protein: 4g | Fat: 8g

INGREDIENTS:

- 500g potatoes, peeled and diced
- 2 leeks, sliced
- 1 onion, chopped
- 2 cloves garlic, minced
- 200ml coconut milk
- 1 litre vegetable broth
- Salt and pepper to taste

INSTRUCTIONS:

1 Place potatoes, sliced leeks, onion, and garlic in the soup maker.

2 Add coconut milk and vegetable broth.

3 Set the soup maker to the "smooth" setting and let it blend and cook.

4 Season with salt and pepper to taste.

5 Serve hot.

20. SPICY TOMATO AND LENTIL SOUP

A zesty and protein-packed vegan soup featuring red lentils and tomatoes.

Nutritional Information (per serving):
Calories: 220 kcal | Carbohydrates: 30g | Protein: 10g | Fat: 2g

INGREDIENTS:

- 200g red lentils
- 400g canned diced tomatoes
- 1 onion, chopped
- 2 cloves garlic, minced
- 1 tsp chilli powder
- 1 litre vegetable broth
- Salt and pepper to taste

INSTRUCTIONS:

1 Place red lentils, diced tomatoes, onion, garlic, and chilli powder in the soup maker.

2 Add vegetable broth.

3 Set the soup maker to the "smooth" setting and let it blend and cook.

4 Season with salt and pepper to taste.

5 Serve hot, garnished with chopped fresh coriander and a squeeze of lime juice.

MEAT SOUP MAKER RECIPES

Meat soups, with their deep flavours and hearty textures, have been central to culinary traditions across the globe. These soups celebrate the rich, robust essence that only meat can impart, creating dishes that are both satisfying to the palate and nourishing to the body.

In this chapter, we'll immerse ourselves in the diverse world of meat-based soups. From the slow-simmered broths that extract every ounce of flavour from bones and cuts to the chunky stews brimming with tender pieces, meat soups epitomise the concept of food as sustenance and comfort.

These recipes underscore the versatility of meat in the realm of soups. The combination of age-old techniques with the efficiency of modern soup makers ensures that these beloved dishes can be recreated with ease and precision.

Join us on this gastronomic journey as we explore the depth and diversity of meat soups, uncovering recipes that have been cherished for generations and introducing innovative twists on timeless classics. Each bowl promises a flavourful voyage, celebrating the rich legacy of meat in culinary traditions.

1. CLASSIC CHICKEN NOODLE SOUP

A comforting and classic chicken noodle soup that's perfect for warming up on chilly days.

Nutritional Information (per serving):
Calories: 250 kcal | Carbohydrates: 15g | Protein: 20g | Fat: 12g

INGREDIENTS:

- 250g chicken breast, diced
- 100g egg noodles
- 1 onion, chopped
- 2 carrots, sliced
- 2 celery stalks, chopped
- 2 cloves garlic, minced
- 1 litre chicken broth
- Salt and pepper to taste

INSTRUCTIONS:

1 Place chicken breast, egg noodles, chopped onion, sliced carrots, chopped celery, and minced garlic in the soup maker.

2 Add chicken broth.

3 Set the soup maker to the "smooth" setting and let it blend and cook.

4 Season with salt and pepper to taste.

5 Serve hot.

2. BEEF AND BARLEY SOUP

A hearty and filling beef and barley soup with rich flavours and tender chunks of beef.

Nutritional Information (per serving):
Calories: 280 kcal | Carbohydrates: 20g | Protein: 24g | Fat: 12g

INGREDIENTS:

- 300g beef stew meat, cubed
- 100g pearl barley
- 1 onion, chopped
- 2 carrots, sliced
- 2 celery stalks, chopped
- 2 cloves garlic, minced
- 1 litre beef broth
- Salt and pepper to taste

INSTRUCTIONS:

1 Place beef stew meat, pearl barley, chopped onion, sliced carrots, chopped celery, and minced garlic in the soup maker.

2 Add beef broth.

3 Set the soup maker to the "smooth" setting and let it blend and cook.

4 Season with salt and pepper to taste.

5 Serve hot.

3. ITALIAN WEDDING SOUP

A delicious Italian wedding soup with mini meatballs, pasta, and fresh greens.

Nutritional Information (per serving):
Calories: 260 kcal | Carbohydrates: 20g | Protein: 18g | Fat: 12g

INGREDIENTS:

- 200g ground pork
- 200g ground beef
- 100g small pasta (e.g., orzo)
- 1 onion, chopped
- 2 carrots, sliced
- 2 celery stalks, chopped
- 2 cloves garlic, minced
- 1 litre chicken broth
- 100g fresh spinach, chopped
- Salt and pepper to taste

INSTRUCTIONS:

1 In a bowl, combine ground pork and ground beef. Form small meatballs and set aside.
2 Place small pasta, chopped onion, sliced carrots, chopped celery, and minced garlic in the soup maker.
3 Add chicken broth and meatballs.
4 Set the soup maker to the "smooth" setting and let it blend and cook.
5 Add chopped fresh spinach and stir until wilted.
6 Season with salt and pepper to taste.
7 Serve hot.

4. SPICY SAUSAGE AND LENTIL SOUP

A spicy and satisfying soup featuring Italian sausage and hearty lentils.

Nutritional Information (per serving):
Calories: 320 kcal | Carbohydrates: 25g | Protein: 18g | Fat: 18g

INGREDIENTS:

- 300g Italian sausage, sliced
- 200g brown lentils
- 1 onion, chopped
- 2 cloves garlic, minced
- 1 red bell pepper, chopped
- 1 tsp red pepper flakes
- 1 litre vegetable broth
- Salt and pepper to taste

INSTRUCTIONS:

1 Place Italian sausage slices, brown lentils, chopped onion, minced garlic, chopped red bell pepper, and red pepper flakes in the soup maker.

2 Add vegetable broth.

3 Set the soup maker to the "smooth" setting and let it blend and cook.

4 Season with salt and pepper to taste.

5 Serve hot.

5. CREAMY POTATO AND BACON SOUP

A creamy and indulgent soup featuring the classic combination of potatoes and crispy bacon.

Nutritional Information (per serving):
Calories: 350 kcal | Carbohydrates: 25g | Protein: 12g | Fat: 22g

INGREDIENTS:

- 200g bacon, chopped
- 500g potatoes, peeled and diced
- 1 onion, chopped
- 2 cloves garlic, minced
- 200ml heavy cream
- 1 litre chicken broth
- Salt and pepper to taste

INSTRUCTIONS:

1 In a pan, cook chopped bacon until crispy. Remove and drain on paper towels.

2 Place diced potatoes, chopped onion, minced garlic, and cooked bacon in the soup maker.

3 Add heavy cream and chicken broth.

4 Set the soup maker to the "smooth" setting and let it blend and cook.

5 Season with salt and pepper to taste.

6 Serve hot.

6. CREAMY MUSHROOM AND BEEF SOUP

A rich and creamy soup featuring tender beef and earthy mushrooms.

Nutritional Information (per serving):
Calories: 320 kcal | Carbohydrates: 15g | Protein: 24g | Fat: 18g

INGREDIENTS:

- 300g beef stew meat, cubed
- 250g mushrooms, sliced
- 1 onion, chopped
- 2 cloves garlic, minced
- 200ml heavy cream
- 1 litre beef broth
- Salt and pepper to taste

INSTRUCTIONS:

1 In a pan, sear beef stew meat until browned. Remove and set aside.
2 Place sliced mushrooms, chopped onion, minced garlic, and seared beef in the soup maker.
3 Add heavy cream and beef broth.
4 Set the soup maker to the "smooth" setting and let it blend and cook.
5 Season with salt and pepper to taste.
6 Serve hot.

7. THAI-INSPIRED CHICKEN AND COCONUT SOUP

A fragrant and creamy Thai-inspired soup with tender chicken and coconut milk.

Nutritional Information (per serving):
Calories: 280 kcal | Carbohydrates: 15g | Protein: 20g | Fat: 15g

INGREDIENTS:

- 250g chicken breast, diced
- 200ml coconut milk
- 1 onion, chopped
- 2 cloves garlic, minced
- 1 thumb-sized piece of ginger, peeled and minced
- 1 tsp red curry paste
- 1 litre chicken broth
- Salt and pepper to taste

INSTRUCTIONS:

1 Place diced chicken breast, coconut milk, chopped onion, minced garlic, minced ginger, and red curry paste in the soup maker.
2 Add chicken broth.
3 Set the soup maker to the "smooth" setting and let it blend and cook.
4 Season with salt and pepper to taste.
5 Serve hot.

8. MOROCCAN LAMB AND CHICKPEA SOUP

A flavorful and aromatic Moroccan-inspired soup featuring tender lamb and chickpeas.

Nutritional Information (per serving):
Calories: 340 kcal | Carbohydrates: 25g | Protein: 22g | Fat: 18g

INGREDIENTS:

- 300g lamb stew meat, cubed
- 200g canned chickpeas, drained and rinsed
- 1 onion, chopped
- 2 cloves garlic, minced
- 1 tsp ground cumin
- 1 tsp ground coriander
- 1 litre vegetable broth
- Salt and pepper to taste

INSTRUCTIONS:

1 In a pan, brown lamb stew meat. Remove and set aside.
2 Place drained chickpeas, chopped onion, minced garlic, ground cumin, ground coriander, and seared lamb in the soup maker.
3 Add vegetable broth.
4 Set the soup maker to the "smooth" setting and let it blend and cook.
5 Season with salt and pepper to taste.
6 Serve hot.

9. SMOKY HAM AND SPLIT PEA SOUP

A smoky and hearty soup featuring chunks of ham and tender split peas.

Nutritional Information (per serving):
Calories: 280 kcal | Carbohydrates: 30g | Protein: 20g | Fat: 10g

INGREDIENTS:

- 250g smoked ham, diced
- 200g split peas
- 1 onion, chopped
- 2 carrots, sliced
- 2 celery stalks, chopped
- 2 cloves garlic, minced
- 1 litre vegetable broth
- Salt and pepper to taste

INSTRUCTIONS:

1. Place diced smoked ham, split peas, chopped onion, sliced carrots, chopped celery, and minced garlic in the soup maker.
2. Add vegetable broth.
3. Set the soup maker to the "smooth" setting and let it blend and cook.
4. Season with salt and pepper to taste.
5. Serve hot.

10. SPICY TURKEY AND RICE SOUP

A spicy and filling soup featuring lean turkey and tender rice.

Nutritional Information (per serving):
Calories: 260 kcal | Carbohydrates: 20g | Protein: 22g | Fat: 10g

INGREDIENTS:

- 250g ground turkey
- 100g rice
- 1 onion, chopped
- 2 cloves garlic, minced
- 1 red bell pepper, chopped
- 1 tsp chilli powder
- 1 litre chicken broth
- Salt and pepper to taste

INSTRUCTIONS:

1. In a pan, brown ground turkey. Remove and set aside.
2. Place rice, chopped onion, minced garlic, chopped red bell pepper, chilli powder, and seared ground turkey in the soup maker.
3. Add chicken broth.
4. Set the soup maker to the "smooth" setting and let it blend and cook.
5. Season with salt and pepper to taste.
6. Serve hot.

11. CREAMY CHICKEN AND MUSHROOM SOUP

A creamy and savoury soup with tender chicken and earthy mushrooms.

Nutritional Information (per serving):
Calories: 280 kcal | Carbohydrates: 15g | Protein: 22g | Fat: 15g

INGREDIENTS:

- 250g chicken breast, diced
- 250g mushrooms, sliced
- 1 onion, chopped
- 2 cloves garlic, minced
- 200ml heavy cream
- 1 litre chicken broth
- Salt and pepper to taste

INSTRUCTIONS:

1 Place diced chicken breast, sliced mushrooms, chopped onion, minced garlic, and heavy cream in the soup maker.
2 Add chicken broth.
3 Set the soup maker to the "smooth" setting and let it blend and cook.
4 Season with salt and pepper to taste.
5 Serve hot.

12. SPICY CHORIZO AND POTATO SOUP

A spicy and hearty soup featuring smoky chorizo and tender potatoes.

Nutritional Information (per serving):
Calories: 340 kcal | Carbohydrates: 20g | Protein: 18g | Fat: 22g

INGREDIENTS:

- 200g chorizo sausage, sliced
- 500g potatoes, peeled and diced
- 1 onion, chopped
- 2 cloves garlic, minced
- 1 tsp paprika
- 1 litre chicken broth
- Salt and pepper to taste

INSTRUCTIONS:

1 In a pan, cook sliced chorizo until crispy. Remove and drain on paper towels.
2 Place diced potatoes, chopped onion, minced garlic, paprika, and cooked chorizo in the soup maker.
3 Add chicken broth.
4 Set the soup maker to the "smooth" setting and let it blend and cook.
5 Season with salt and pepper to taste.
6 Serve hot.

13. TOP TURKEY AND WILD RICE SOUP

A creamy and satisfying soup with tender turkey and nutty wild rice.

Nutritional Information (per serving):
Calories: 320 kcal | Carbohydrates: 25g | Protein: 24g | Fat: 15g

INGREDIENTS:

- 250g cooked turkey, diced
- 100g wild rice, cooked
- 1 onion, chopped
- 2 carrots, sliced
- 2 celery stalks, chopped
- 2 cloves garlic, minced
- 200ml heavy cream
- 1 litre chicken broth
- Salt and pepper to taste

INSTRUCTIONS:

1 Place diced cooked turkey, cooked wild rice, chopped onion, sliced carrots, chopped celery, and minced garlic in the soup maker.
2 Add heavy cream and chicken broth.
3 Set the soup maker to the "smooth" setting and let it blend and cook.
4 Season with salt and pepper to taste.
5 Serve hot.

14. CREAMY BACON AND POTATO SOUP

A creamy and indulgent soup with the classic combination of potatoes and crispy bacon.

Nutritional Information (per serving):
Calories: 350 kcal | Carbohydrates: 20g | Protein: 15g | Fat: 25g

INGREDIENTS:

- 200g bacon, chopped
- 500g potatoes, peeled and diced
- 1 onion, chopped
- 2 cloves garlic, minced
- 200ml heavy cream
- 1 litre chicken broth
- Salt and pepper to taste

INSTRUCTIONS:

1 In a pan, cook chopped bacon until crispy. Remove and drain on paper towels.
2 Place diced potatoes, chopped onion, minced garlic, and cooked bacon in the soup maker.
3 Add heavy cream and chicken broth.
4 Set the soup maker to the "smooth" setting and let it blend and cook.
5 Season with salt and pepper to taste.
6 Serve hot.

15. SPICY MEXICAN CHICKEN SOUP

A zesty and flavorful soup with tender chicken and a hint of Mexican spices.

Nutritional Information (per serving):
Calories: 290 kcal | Carbohydrates: 20g | Protein: 22g | Fat: 15g

INGREDIENTS:

- 250g chicken breast, diced
- 1 onion, chopped
- 2 cloves garlic, minced
- 1 red bell pepper, chopped
- 1 tsp chilli powder
- 1 tsp cumin
- 1 litre chicken broth
- Salt and pepper to taste

INSTRUCTIONS:

1 Place diced chicken breast, chopped onion, minced garlic, chopped red bell pepper, chilli powder, and cumin in the soup maker.
2 Add chicken broth.
3 Set the soup maker to the "smooth" setting and let it blend and cook.
4 Season with salt and pepper to taste.
5 Serve hot, garnished with chopped fresh coriander and a squeeze of lime juice.

16. CREAMY TOMATO AND SAUSAGE SOUP

A creamy and savoury soup featuring Italian sausage and tangy tomatoes.

Nutritional Information (per serving):
Calories: 330 kcal | Carbohydrates: 20g | Protein: 18g | Fat: 20g

INGREDIENTS:

- 200g Italian sausage, sliced
- 500g ripe tomatoes, halved
- 1 onion, chopped
- 2 cloves garlic, minced
- 200ml heavy cream
- 1 litre chicken broth
- Salt and pepper to taste

INSTRUCTIONS:

1 In a pan, cook sliced Italian sausage until browned. Remove and set aside.

2 Place ripe tomatoes, chopped onion, minced garlic, and cooked sausage in the soup maker.

3 Add heavy cream and chicken broth.

4 Set the soup maker to the "smooth" setting and let it blend and cook.

5 Season with salt and pepper to taste.

6 Serve hot.

17. CREAMY HAM AND POTATO SOUP

A creamy and comforting soup with tender chunks of ham and hearty potatoes.

Nutritional Information (per serving):
Calories: 320 kcal | Carbohydrates: 25g | Protein: 18g | Fat: 18g

INGREDIENTS:

- 250g cooked ham, diced
- 500g potatoes, peeled and diced
- 1 onion, chopped
- 2 cloves garlic, minced
- 200ml heavy cream
- 1 litre chicken broth
- Salt and pepper to taste

INSTRUCTIONS:

1 Place diced cooked ham, diced potatoes, chopped onion, minced garlic, and heavy cream in the soup maker.

2 Add chicken broth.

3 Set the soup maker to the "smooth" setting and let it blend and cook.

4 Season with salt and pepper to taste.

5 Serve hot.

18. SPICY CAJUN SAUSAGE AND RICE SOUP

A spicy and flavorful soup featuring Cajun sausage and tender rice.

Nutritional Information (per serving):
Calories: 340 kcal | Carbohydrates: 25g | Protein: 18g | Fat: 20g

INGREDIENTS:

- 200g Cajun sausage, sliced
- 100g rice
- 1 onion, chopped
- 2 cloves garlic, minced
- 1 red bell pepper, chopped
- 1 tsp Cajun seasoning
- 1 litre chicken broth
- Salt and pepper to taste

INSTRUCTIONS:

1. In a pan, cook sliced Cajun sausage until browned. Remove and set aside.
2. Place rice, chopped onion, minced garlic, chopped red bell pepper, Cajun seasoning, and cooked sausage in the soup maker.
3. Add chicken broth.
4. Set the soup maker to the "smooth" setting and let it blend and cook.
5. Season with salt and pepper to taste.
6. Serve hot.

19. CREAMY TURKEY AND MUSHROOM SOUP

A creamy and savoury soup featuring tender turkey and earthy mushrooms.

Nutritional Information (per serving):
Calories: 290 kcal | Carbohydrates: 20g | Protein: 22g | Fat: 16g

INGREDIENTS:

- 250g cooked turkey, diced
- 250g mushrooms, sliced
- 1 onion, chopped
- 2 cloves garlic, minced
- 200ml heavy cream
- 1 litre chicken broth
- Salt and pepper to taste

INSTRUCTIONS:

1. Place diced cooked turkey, sliced mushrooms, chopped onion, minced garlic, and heavy cream in the soup maker.
2. Add chicken broth.
3. Set the soup maker to the "smooth" setting and let it blend and cook.
4. Season with salt and pepper to taste.
5. Serve hot.

20. CREAMY CORN AND BACON CHOWDER

A creamy and indulgent chowder featuring sweet corn and crispy bacon.

Nutritional Information (per serving):
Calories: 350 kcal | Carbohydrates: 25g | Protein: 12g | Fat: 22g

INGREDIENTS:

- 200g bacon, chopped
- 500g sweet corn kernels (fresh or frozen)
- 1 onion, chopped
- 2 cloves garlic, minced
- 200ml heavy cream
- 1 litre chicken broth
- Salt and pepper to taste

INSTRUCTIONS:

1 In a pan, cook chopped bacon until crispy. Remove and drain on paper towels.

2 Place sweet corn kernels, chopped onion, minced garlic, and cooked bacon in the soup maker.

3 Add heavy cream and chicken broth.

4 Set the soup maker to the "smooth" setting and let it blend and cook.

5 Season with salt and pepper to taste.

6 Serve hot.

21. HEARTY BEEF AND VEGETABLE SOUP

A hearty and nutritious soup with tender beef and a variety of vegetables.

Nutritional Information (per serving):
Calories: 280 kcal | Carbohydrates: 20g | Protein: 20g | Fat: 15g

INGREDIENTS:

- 300g beef stew meat, cubed
- 2 carrots, sliced
- 2 celery stalks, chopped
- 2 potatoes, peeled and diced
- 1 onion, chopped
- 2 cloves garlic, minced
- 1 litre beef broth
- Salt and pepper to taste

INSTRUCTIONS:

1 Place beef stew meat, sliced carrots, chopped celery, diced potatoes, chopped onion, and minced garlic in the soup maker.

2 Add beef broth.

3 Set the soup maker to the "smooth" setting and let it blend and cook.

4 Season with salt and pepper to taste.

5 Serve hot.

22. CLASSIC CHICKEN AND LEEK SOUP

A creamy and flavorful soup with tender chicken and the subtle sweetness of leeks.

Nutritional Information (per serving):
Calories: 270 kcal | Carbohydrates: 15g | Protein: 20g | Fat: 15g

INGREDIENTS:
- 250g chicken breast, diced
- 2 leeks, white and light green parts, sliced
- 1 onion, chopped
- 2 cloves garlic, minced
- 200ml heavy cream
- 1 litre chicken broth
- Salt and pepper to taste

INSTRUCTIONS:
1. Place diced chicken breast, sliced leeks, chopped onion, minced garlic, and heavy cream in the soup maker.
2. Add chicken broth.
3. Set the soup maker to the "smooth" setting and let it blend and cook.
4. Season with salt and pepper to taste.
5. Serve hot.

23. CREAMY TOMATO AND BEEF SOUP

A creamy and satisfying soup with tender beef and tangy tomatoes.

Nutritional Information (per serving):
Calories: 330 kcal | Carbohydrates: 20g | Protein: 18g | Fat: 20g

INGREDIENTS:
- 300g beef stew meat, cubed
- 500g ripe tomatoes, halved
- 1 onion, chopped
- 2 cloves garlic, minced
- 200ml heavy cream
- 1 litre beef broth
- Salt and pepper to taste

INSTRUCTIONS:
1. In a pan, sear beef stew meat until browned. Remove and set aside.
2. Place ripe tomatoes, chopped onion, minced garlic, and seared beef in the soup maker.
3. Add heavy cream and beef broth.
4. Set the soup maker to the "smooth" setting and let it blend and cook.
5. Season with salt and pepper to taste.
6. Serve hot.

24. SPICY CHORIZO AND BEAN SOUP

A spicy and flavorful soup featuring smoky chorizo and hearty beans.

Nutritional Information (per serving):
Calories: 320 kcal | Carbohydrates: 25g | Protein: 16g | Fat: 18g

INGREDIENTS:

- 200g chorizo sausage, sliced
- 400g canned kidney beans, drained and rinsed
- 1 onion, chopped
- 2 cloves garlic, minced
- 1 red bell pepper, chopped
- 1 tsp smoked paprika
- 1 litre chicken broth
- Salt and pepper to taste

INSTRUCTIONS:

1 In a pan, cook sliced chorizo until crispy. Remove and drain on paper towels.
2 Place drained kidney beans, chopped onion, minced garlic, chopped red bell pepper, smoked paprika, and cooked chorizo in the soup maker.
3 Add chicken broth.
4 Set the soup maker to the "smooth" setting and let it blend and cook.
5 Season with salt and pepper to taste.
6 Serve hot.

25. CREAMY TURKEY AND VEGETABLE SOUP

A creamy and wholesome soup with tender turkey and a medley of vegetables.

Nutritional Information (per serving):
Calories: 270 kcal | Carbohydrates: 20g | Protein: 20g | Fat: 15g

INGREDIENTS:

- 250g cooked turkey, diced
- 2 carrots, sliced
- 2 celery stalks, chopped
- 2 potatoes, peeled and diced
- 1 onion, chopped
- 2 cloves garlic, minced
- 200ml heavy cream
- 1 litre chicken broth
- Salt and pepper to taste

INSTRUCTIONS:

1 Place diced cooked turkey, sliced carrots, chopped celery, diced potatoes, chopped onion, and minced garlic in the soup maker.

2 Add heavy cream and chicken broth.

3 Set the soup maker to the "smooth" setting and let it blend and cook.

4 Season with salt and pepper to taste.

5 Serve hot.

26. CLASSIC MUSHROOM AND CHICKEN SOUP

A creamy and savoury soup featuring tender chicken and earthy mushrooms.

Nutritional Information (per serving):
Calories: 280 kcal | Carbohydrates: 15g | Protein: 20g | Fat: 16g

INGREDIENTS:

- 250g chicken breast, diced
- 250g mushrooms, sliced
- 1 onion, chopped
- 2 cloves garlic, minced
- 200ml heavy cream
- 1 litre chicken broth
- Salt and pepper to taste

INSTRUCTIONS:

1 Place diced chicken breast, sliced mushrooms, chopped onion, minced garlic, and heavy cream in the soup maker.

2 Add chicken broth.

3 Set the soup maker to the "smooth" setting and let it blend and cook.

4 Season with salt and pepper to taste.

5 Serve hot.

27. CREAMY TOMATO AND TURKEY SOUP

A creamy and satisfying soup with tender turkey and tangy tomatoes.

Nutritional Information (per serving):
Calories: 320 kcal | Carbohydrates: 20g | Protein: 18g | Fat: 18g

INGREDIENTS:

- 250g cooked turkey, diced
- 500g ripe tomatoes, halved
- 1 onion, chopped
- 2 cloves garlic, minced
- 200ml heavy cream
- 1 litre chicken broth
- Salt and pepper to taste

INSTRUCTIONS:

1 Place diced cooked turkey, ripe tomatoes, chopped onion, minced garlic, and heavy cream in the soup maker.

2 Add chicken broth.

3 Set the soup maker to the "smooth" setting and let it blend and cook.

4 Season with salt and pepper to taste.

5 Serve hot.

28. CHICKEN AND SPINACH SOUP

A creamy and nutritious soup with tender chicken and vibrant spinach.

Nutritional Information (per serving):
Calories: 270 kcal | Carbohydrates: 15g | Protein: 20g | Fat: 15g

INGREDIENTS:

- 250g chicken breast, diced
- 100g fresh spinach, chopped
- 1 onion, chopped
- 2 cloves garlic, minced
- 200ml heavy cream
- 1 litre chicken broth
- Salt and pepper to taste

INSTRUCTIONS:

1 Place diced chicken breast, chopped fresh spinach, chopped onion, minced garlic, and heavy cream in the soup maker.

2 Add chicken broth.

3 Set the soup maker to the "smooth" setting and let it blend and cook.

4 Season with salt and pepper to taste.

5 Serve hot.

29. TURKEY AND BACON SOUP

A creamy and indulgent soup featuring tender turkey and crispy bacon.

Nutritional Information (per serving):
Calories: 320 kcal | Carbohydrates: 20g | Protein: 18g | Fat: 18g

INGREDIENTS:

- 250g cooked turkey, diced
- 200g bacon, chopped
- 1 onion, chopped
- 2 cloves garlic, minced
- 200ml heavy cream
- 1 litre chicken broth
- Salt and pepper to taste

INSTRUCTIONS:

1 In a pan, cook chopped bacon until crispy. Remove and drain on paper towels.
2 Place diced cooked turkey, chopped bacon, chopped onion, minced garlic, and heavy cream in the soup maker.
3 Add chicken broth.
4 Set the soup maker to the "smooth" setting and let it blend and cook.
5 Season with salt and pepper to taste.
6 Serve hot.

30. CREAMY MUSHROOM AND HAM SOUP

A creamy and savoury soup featuring earthy mushrooms and chunks of ham.

Nutritional Information (per serving):
Calories: 290 kcal | Carbohydrates: 15g | Protein: 18g | Fat: 16g

INGREDIENTS:

- 250g ham, diced
- 250g mushrooms, sliced
- 1 onion, chopped
- 2 cloves garlic, minced
- 200ml heavy cream
- 1 litre chicken broth
- Salt and pepper to taste

INSTRUCTIONS:

1 Place diced ham, sliced mushrooms, chopped onion, minced garlic, and heavy cream in the soup maker.
2 Add chicken broth.
3 Set the soup maker to the "smooth" setting and let it blend and cook.
4 Season with salt and pepper to taste.
5 Serve hot.

31. CHICKEN AND BROCCOLI SOUP

A creamy and nutritious soup with tender chicken and vibrant broccoli.

Nutritional Information (per serving):
Calories: 280 kcal | Carbohydrates: 15g | Protein: 20g | Fat: 15g

INGREDIENTS:

- 250g chicken breast, diced
- 200g broccoli florets
- 1 onion, chopped
- 2 cloves garlic, minced
- 200ml heavy cream
- 1 litre chicken broth
- Salt and pepper to taste

INSTRUCTIONS:

1 Place diced chicken breast, broccoli florets, chopped onion, minced garlic, and heavy cream in the soup maker.

2 Add chicken broth.

3 Set the soup maker to the "smooth" setting and let it blend and cook.

4 Season with salt and pepper to taste.

5 Serve hot.

32. CLASSIC TOMATO AND BACON SOUP

A creamy and indulgent soup with the classic combination of tomatoes and crispy bacon.

Nutritional Information (per serving):
Calories: 340 kcal | Carbohydrates: 20g | Protein: 15g | Fat: 22g

INGREDIENTS:

- 200g bacon, chopped
- 500g ripe tomatoes, halved
- 1 onion, chopped
- 2 cloves garlic, minced
- 200ml heavy cream
- 1 litre chicken broth
- Salt and pepper to taste

INSTRUCTIONS:

1 In a pan, cook chopped bacon until crispy. Remove and drain on paper towels.

2 Place ripe tomatoes, chopped onion, minced garlic, and cooked bacon in the soup maker.

3 Add heavy cream and chicken broth.

4 Set the soup maker to the "smooth" setting and let it blend and cook.

5 Season with salt and pepper to taste.

6 Serve hot.

33. CREAMY CHICKEN AND CORN SOUP

A creamy and satisfying soup with tender chicken and sweet corn.

Nutritional Information (per serving):
Calories: 270 kcal | Carbohydrates: 15g | Protein: 20g | Fat: 15g

INGREDIENTS:
- 250g chicken breast, diced
- 200g sweet corn kernels (fresh or frozen)
- 1 onion, chopped
- 2 cloves garlic, minced
- 200ml heavy cream
- 1 litre chicken broth
- Salt and pepper to taste

INSTRUCTIONS:
1. Place diced chicken breast, sweet corn kernels, chopped onion, minced garlic, and heavy cream in the soup maker.
2. Add chicken broth.
3. Set the soup maker to the "smooth" setting and let it blend and cook.
4. Season with salt and pepper to taste.
5. Serve hot.

34. HEARTY BEEF AND BROCCOLI SOUP

A creamy and nutritious soup with tender beef and vibrant broccoli.

Nutritional Information (per serving):
Calories: 280 kcal | Carbohydrates: 15g | Protein: 20g | Fat: 15g

INGREDIENTS:
- 300g beef stew meat, cubed
- 200g broccoli florets
- 1 onion, chopped
- 2 cloves garlic, minced
- 200ml heavy cream
- 1 litre beef broth
- Salt and pepper to taste

INSTRUCTIONS:
1. Place beef stew meat, broccoli florets, chopped onion, minced garlic, and heavy cream in the soup maker.
2. Add beef broth.
3. Set the soup maker to the "smooth" setting and let it blend and cook.
4. Season with salt and pepper to taste.
5. Serve hot.

35. SUPERB TOMATO AND SAUSAGE SOUP

A creamy and savoury soup featuring Italian sausage and tangy tomatoes.

Nutritional Information (per serving):
Calories: 330 kcal | Carbohydrates: 20g | Protein: 18g | Fat: 20g

INGREDIENTS:
- 200g Italian sausage, sliced
- 500g ripe tomatoes, halved
- 1 onion, chopped
- 2 cloves garlic, minced
- 200ml heavy cream
- 1 litre chicken broth
- Salt and pepper to taste

INSTRUCTIONS:
1 In a pan, cook sliced Italian sausage until browned. Remove and set aside.
2 Place ripe tomatoes, chopped onion, minced garlic, and cooked sausage in the soup maker.
3 Add heavy cream and chicken broth.
4 Set the soup maker to the "smooth" setting and let it blend and cook.
5 Season with salt and pepper to taste.
6 Serve hot.

36. CREAMY HAM AND LEEK SOUP

A creamy and flavorful soup with chunks of ham and the subtle sweetness of leeks.

Nutritional Information (per serving):
Calories: 290 kcal | Carbohydrates: 15g | Protein: 18g | Fat: 16g

INGREDIENTS:
- 250g ham, diced
- 2 leeks, white and light green parts, sliced
- 1 onion, chopped
- 2 cloves garlic, minced
- 200ml heavy cream
- 1 litre chicken broth
- Salt and pepper to taste

INSTRUCTIONS:
1 Place diced ham, sliced leeks, chopped onion, minced garlic, and heavy cream in the soup maker.
2 Add chicken broth.
3 Set the soup maker to the "smooth" setting and let it blend and cook.
4 Season with salt and pepper to taste.
5 Serve hot.

37. CLASSIC CHICKEN AND ASPARAGUS SOUP

A creamy and nutritious soup with tender chicken and fresh asparagus.

Nutritional Information (per serving):
Calories: 270 kcal | Carbohydrates: 15g | Protein: 20g | Fat: 15g

INGREDIENTS:

- 250g chicken breast, diced
- 200g fresh asparagus spears, chopped
- 1 onion, chopped
- 2 cloves garlic, minced
- 200ml heavy cream
- 1 litre chicken broth
- Salt and pepper to taste

INSTRUCTIONS:

1 Place diced chicken breast, chopped fresh asparagus spears, chopped onion, minced garlic, and heavy cream in the soup maker.

2 Add chicken broth.

3 Set the soup maker to the "smooth" setting and let it blend and cook.

4 Season with salt and pepper to taste.

5 Serve hot.

38. CREAMY TURKEY AND SPINACH SOUP

A creamy and nutritious soup with tender turkey and vibrant spinach.

Nutritional Information (per serving):
Calories: 280 kcal | Carbohydrates: 15g | Protein: 20g | Fat: 15g

INGREDIENTS:

- 250g cooked turkey, diced
- 100g fresh spinach, chopped
- 1 onion, chopped
- 2 cloves garlic, minced
- 200ml heavy cream
- 1 litre chicken broth
- Salt and pepper to taste

INSTRUCTIONS:

1 Place diced cooked turkey, chopped fresh spinach, chopped onion, minced garlic, and heavy cream in the soup maker.

2 Add chicken broth.

3 Set the soup maker to the "smooth" setting and let it blend and cook.

4 Season with salt and pepper to taste.

5 Serve hot.

39. CREAMY TOMATO AND MUSHROOM SOUP

A creamy and savoury soup featuring tangy tomatoes and earthy mushrooms.

Nutritional Information (per serving):
Calories: 320 kcal | Carbohydrates: 20g | Protein: 15g | Fat: 18g

INGREDIENTS:
- 500g ripe tomatoes, halved
- 250g mushrooms, sliced
- 1 onion, chopped
- 2 cloves garlic, minced
- 200ml heavy cream
- 1 litre chicken broth
- Salt and pepper to taste

INSTRUCTIONS:
1. Place ripe tomatoes, sliced mushrooms, chopped onion, minced garlic, and heavy cream in the soup maker.
2. Add chicken broth.
3. Set the soup maker to the "smooth" setting and let it blend and cook.
4. Season with salt and pepper to taste.
5. Serve hot.

40. TURKEY AND LEEK SOUP

A creamy and flavorful soup with tender turkey and the subtle sweetness of leeks.

Nutritional Information (per serving):
Calories: 290 kcal | Carbohydrates: 15g | Protein: 18g | Fat: 16g

INGREDIENTS:
- 250g cooked turkey, diced
- 2 leeks, white and light green parts, sliced
- 1 onion, chopped
- 2 cloves garlic, minced
- 200ml heavy cream
- 1 litre chicken broth
- Salt and pepper to taste

INSTRUCTIONS:
1. Place diced cooked turkey, sliced leeks, chopped onion, minced garlic, and heavy cream in the soup maker.
2. Add chicken broth.
3. Set the soup maker to the "smooth" setting and let it blend and cook.
4. Season with salt and pepper to taste.
5. Serve hot.

41. DELICIOUS CHICKEN AND BELL PEPPER SOUP

A creamy and vibrant soup with tender chicken and colourful bell peppers.

Nutritional Information (per serving):
Calories: 270 kcal | Carbohydrates: 15g | Protein: 20g | Fat: 15g

INGREDIENTS:
- 250g chicken breast, diced
- 2 bell peppers (any colour), chopped
- 1 onion, chopped
- 2 cloves garlic, minced
- 200ml heavy cream
- 1 litre chicken broth
- Salt and pepper to taste

INSTRUCTIONS:
1. Place diced chicken breast, chopped bell peppers, chopped onion, minced garlic, and heavy cream in the soup maker.
2. Add chicken broth.
3. Set the soup maker to the "smooth" setting and let it blend and cook.
4. Season with salt and pepper to taste.
5. Serve hot.

42. CREAMY TURKEY AND BELL PEPPER SOUP

A creamy and vibrant soup with tender turkey and colourful bell peppers.

Nutritional Information (per serving):
Calories: 270 kcal | Carbohydrates: 15g | Protein: 20g | Fat: 15g

INGREDIENTS:
- 250g cooked turkey, diced
- 2 bell peppers (any colour), chopped
- 1 onion, chopped
- 2 cloves garlic, minced
- 200ml heavy cream
- 1 litre chicken broth
- Salt and pepper to taste

INSTRUCTIONS:
1. Place diced cooked turkey, chopped bell peppers, chopped onion, minced garlic, and heavy cream in the soup maker.
2. Add chicken broth.
3. Set the soup maker to the "smooth" setting and let it blend and cook.
4. Season with salt and pepper to taste.
5. Serve hot.

43. HEARTY TOMATO AND CHORIZO SOUP

A creamy and flavorful soup with smoky chorizo and tangy tomatoes.

Nutritional Information (per serving):
Calories: 330 kcal | Carbohydrates: 20g | Protein: 18g | Fat: 20g

INGREDIENTS:

- 200g chorizo sausage, sliced
- 500g ripe tomatoes, halved
- 1 onion, chopped
- 2 cloves garlic, minced
- 200ml heavy cream
- 1 litre chicken broth
- Salt and pepper to taste

INSTRUCTIONS:

1 In a pan, cook sliced chorizo until crispy. Remove and drain on paper towels.
2 Place ripe tomatoes, chopped onion, minced garlic, and cooked chorizo in the soup maker.
3 Add heavy cream and chicken broth.
4 Set the soup maker to the "smooth" setting and let it blend and cook.
5 Season with salt and pepper to taste.
6 Serve hot.

44. CREAMY TURKEY AND BELL PEPPER SOUP

A creamy and vibrant soup with tender turkey and colourful bell peppers.

Nutritional Information (per serving):
Calories: 270 kcal | Carbohydrates: 15g | Protein: 20g | Fat: 15g

INGREDIENTS:

- 250g cooked turkey, diced
- 2 bell peppers (any colour), chopped
- 1 onion, chopped
- 2 cloves garlic, minced
- 200ml heavy cream
- 1 litre chicken broth
- Salt and pepper to taste

INSTRUCTIONS:

1 Place diced cooked turkey, chopped bell peppers, chopped onion, minced garlic, and heavy cream in the soup maker.
2 Add chicken broth.
3 Set the soup maker to the "smooth" setting and let it blend and cook.
4 Season with salt and pepper to taste.
5 Serve hot.

45. SUPER TOMATO AND CHORIZO SOUP

A creamy and flavorful soup with smoky chorizo and tangy tomatoes.

Nutritional Information (per serving):
Calories: 330 kcal | Carbohydrates: 20g | Protein: 18g | Fat: 20g

INGREDIENTS:

- 200g chorizo sausage, sliced
- 500g ripe tomatoes, halved
- 1 onion, chopped
- 2 cloves garlic, minced
- 200ml heavy cream
- 1 litre chicken broth
- Salt and pepper to taste

INSTRUCTIONS:

1 In a pan, cook sliced chorizo until crispy. Remove and drain on paper towels.

2 Place ripe tomatoes, chopped onion, minced garlic, and cooked chorizo in the soup maker.

3 Add heavy cream and chicken broth.

4 Set the soup maker to the "smooth" setting and let it blend and cook.

5 Season with salt and pepper to taste.

6 Serve hot.

46. HAM AND BELL PEPPER SOUP

A creamy and vibrant soup with chunks of ham and colourful bell peppers.

Nutritional Information (per serving):
Calories: 290 kcal | Carbohydrates: 15g | Protein: 18g | Fat: 16g

INGREDIENTS:

- 250g ham, diced
- 2 bell peppers (any colour), chopped
- 1 onion, chopped
- 2 cloves garlic, minced
- 200ml heavy cream
- 1 litre chicken broth
- Salt and pepper to taste

INSTRUCTIONS:

1 Place diced ham, chopped bell peppers, chopped onion, minced garlic, and heavy cream in the soup maker.

2 Add chicken broth.

3 Set the soup maker to the "smooth" setting and let it blend and cook.

4 Season with salt and pepper to taste.

5 Serve hot.

47. CREAMY TURKEY AND ASPARAGUS SOUP

A creamy and nutritious soup with tender turkey and fresh asparagus.

Nutritional Information (per serving):

Calories: 280 kcal | Carbohydrates: 15g | Protein: 20g | Fat: 15g

INGREDIENTS:

- 250g cooked turkey, diced
- 200g fresh asparagus spears, chopped
- 1 onion, chopped
- 2 cloves garlic, minced
- 200ml heavy cream
- 1 litre chicken broth
- Salt and pepper to taste

INSTRUCTIONS:

1 Place diced cooked turkey, chopped fresh asparagus spears, chopped onion, minced garlic, and heavy cream in the soup maker.
2 Add chicken broth.
3 Set the soup maker to the "smooth" setting and let it blend and cook.
4 Season with salt and pepper to taste.
5 Serve hot.

48. JUICY TOMATO AND MUSHROOM SOUP

A creamy and savoury soup featuring tangy tomatoes and earthy mushrooms.

Nutritional Information (per serving):

Calories: 320 kcal | Carbohydrates: 20g | Protein: 15g | Fat: 18g

INGREDIENTS:

- 500g ripe tomatoes, halved
- 250g mushrooms, sliced
- 1 onion, chopped
- 2 cloves garlic, minced
- 200ml heavy cream
- 1 litre chicken broth
- Salt and pepper to taste

INSTRUCTIONS:

1 Place ripe tomatoes, sliced mushrooms, chopped onion, minced garlic, and heavy cream in the soup maker.
2 Add chicken broth.
3 Set the soup maker to the "smooth" setting and let it blend and cook.
4 Season with salt and pepper to taste.
5 Serve hot.

49. CREAMY TURKEY AND HAM SOUP

A creamy and indulgent soup featuring tender turkey and chunks of ham.

Nutritional Information (per serving):
Calories: 320 kcal | Carbohydrates: 20g | Protein: 18g | Fat: 18g

INGREDIENTS:

- 250g cooked turkey, diced
- 250g ham, diced
- 1 onion, chopped
- 2 cloves garlic, minced
- 200ml heavy cream
- 1 litre chicken broth
- Salt and pepper to taste

INSTRUCTIONS:

1 Place diced cooked turkey, diced ham, chopped onion, minced garlic, and heavy cream in the soup maker.

2 Add chicken broth.

3 Set the soup maker to the "smooth" setting and let it blend and cook.

4 Season with salt and pepper to taste.

5 Serve hot.

50. CLASSIC CHICKEN AND POTATO SOUP

A creamy and comforting soup with tender chicken and hearty potatoes.

Nutritional Information (per serving):
Calories: 290 kcal | Carbohydrates: 20g | Protein: 20g | Fat: 15g

INGREDIENTS:

- 250g chicken breast, diced
- 500g potatoes, peeled and diced
- 1 onion, chopped
- 2 cloves garlic, minced
- 200ml heavy cream
- 1 litre chicken broth
- Salt and pepper to taste

INSTRUCTIONS:

1 Place diced chicken breast, diced potatoes, chopped onion, minced garlic, and heavy cream in the soup maker.

2 Add chicken broth.

3 Set the soup maker to the "smooth" setting and let it blend and cook.

4 Season with salt and pepper to taste.

5 Serve hot.

SUPERFOOD SOUP MAKER RECIPES

Superfoods, celebrated for their dense nutritional profiles and myriad health benefits, seamlessly blend the worlds of wellness and taste. When incorporated into soups, these powerhouse ingredients create dishes that not only satiate hunger but also nourish the body at its core.

In this chapter, we'll journey through the enticing spectrum of superfood soups. These aren't merely meals; they're elixirs brimming with vitamins, minerals, antioxidants, and flavours that elevate the everyday soup experience. From the antioxidant-rich berry blends to the invigorating green soups powered by leafy vegetables and algae, superfood soups provide a wholesome embrace in every spoonful.

With the integration of modern soup makers, crafting these nutrient-dense concoctions has never been more straightforward or satisfying.

So, let's embark on this healthful adventure, delving into soups that are as beneficial for your well-being as they are delightful to the palate. Here, culinary creativity meets nutritional science, presenting you with a collection of soups that are genuinely super in every sense.

1. SWEET POTATO AND LEEK SOUP

Indulge in the creamy goodness of sweet potato and leek soup. The natural sweetness of sweet potatoes and the mild flavour of leeks make this a delightful choice.

Nutritional Information (per serving):
Calories: 180 kcal | Carbohydrates: 25g | Protein: 4g | Fat: 7g

INGREDIENTS:

- 400g sweet potatoes, peeled and diced
- 2 leeks, sliced
- 2 cloves garlic, minced
- 1 litre vegetable broth
- 15ml olive oil
- Salt and pepper to taste

INSTRUCTIONS:

1. Sauté leeks and garlic in olive oil until softened.
2. Add sweet potatoes and vegetable broth.
3. Cook until sweet potatoes are tender.
4. Blend until smooth.
5. Season with salt and pepper.
6. Serve hot.

2. CAULIFLOWER AND CHICKPEA SOUP

Savour the goodness of cauliflower and chickpea soup. The creamy texture of cauliflower and the protein-packed chickpeas make this soup a satisfying meal.

Nutritional Information (per serving):
Calories: 160 kcal | Carbohydrates: 20g | Protein: 7g | Fat: 6g

INGREDIENTS:

- 400g cauliflower florets
- 200g canned chickpeas, drained and rinsed
- 1 onion, chopped
- 2 cloves garlic, minced

INSTRUCTIONS:

1. Sauté onion and garlic until softened.
2. Add cauliflower, chickpeas, and vegetable broth.
3. Cook until the cauliflower is tender.
4. Blend until smooth.
5. Season with salt and pepper.
6. Serve hot.

3. TOMATO AND RED PEPPER SOUP

Enjoy the vibrant flavours of tomato and red pepper soup. The combination of ripe tomatoes and roasted red peppers creates a delightful balance.

Nutritional Information (per serving):
Calories: 140 kcal | Carbohydrates: 20g | Protein: 3g | Fat: 5g

INGREDIENTS:

- 500g ripe tomatoes, chopped
- 2 red bell peppers, roasted and chopped
- 1 onion, chopped
- 2 cloves garlic, minced
- 1 litre vegetable broth
- 15ml olive oil
- Salt and pepper to taste

INSTRUCTIONS:

1 Sauté onion and garlic in olive oil until translucent.
2 Add chopped tomatoes, roasted red peppers, and vegetable broth.
3 Cook until tomatoes are soft.
4 Blend until smooth.
5 Season with salt and pepper.
6 Serve hot.

4. QUINOA AND KALE SOUP

Fuel your day with quinoa and kale soup. This protein-packed soup combines the nutritional benefits of quinoa and the goodness of kale.

Nutritional Information (per serving):
Calories: 170 kcal | Carbohydrates: 25g | Protein: 7g | Fat: 5g

INGREDIENTS:

- 150g quinoa
- 200g kale leaves, stemmed and chopped
- 1 onion, chopped
- 2 cloves garlic, minced
- 1 litre vegetable broth
- 15ml olive oil
- Salt and pepper to taste

INSTRUCTIONS:

1 Sauté onion and garlic in olive oil until softened.

2 Add quinoa, kale, and vegetable broth.

3 Cook until quinoa is tender.

4 Season with salt and pepper.

5 Serve hot.

5. BEETROOT AND CARROT SOUP

Experience the vibrant colours and flavours of beetroot and carrot soup. This nutritious blend is as visually appealing as it is delicious.

Nutritional Information (per serving):
Calories: 150 kcal | Carbohydrates: 30g | Protein: 3g | Fat: 2g

INGREDIENTS:

- 300g beetroot, peeled and diced
- 300g carrots, peeled and diced
- 1 onion, chopped
- 2 cloves garlic, minced
- 1 litre vegetable broth
- 15ml olive oil
- Salt and pepper to taste

INSTRUCTIONS:

1 Sauté onion and garlic in olive oil until softened.

2 Add diced beetroot, carrots, and vegetable broth.

3 Cook until vegetables are tender.

4 Blend until smooth.

5 Season with salt and pepper.

6 Serve hot.

6. SPINACH AND CHICKPEA SOUP

Elevate your meal with spinach and chickpea soup. The combination of leafy spinach and protein-rich chickpeas makes this soup a nutritional powerhouse.

Nutritional Information (per serving):
Calories: 160 kcal | Carbohydrates: 20g | Protein: 7g | Fat: 6g

INGREDIENTS:

- 200g fresh spinach
- 200g canned chickpeas, drained and rinsed
- 1 onion, chopped
- 2 cloves garlic, minced
- 1 litre vegetable broth
- 15ml olive oil
- Salt and pepper to taste

INSTRUCTIONS:

1. Sauté onion and garlic in olive oil until softened.
2. Add fresh spinach, chickpeas, and vegetable broth.
3. Cook until spinach wilts.
4. Blend until smooth.
5. Season with salt and pepper.
6. Serve hot.

7. LENTIL AND TOMATO SOUP

Get your daily dose of protein with lentil and tomato soup. Packed with red lentils and ripe tomatoes, it's a hearty and nutritious choice.

Nutritional Information (per serving):
Calories: 180 kcal | Carbohydrates: 25g | Protein: 8g | Fat: 5g

INGREDIENTS:

- 200g red lentils
- 500g ripe tomatoes, chopped
- 1 onion, chopped
- 2 cloves garlic, minced
- 1 litre vegetable broth
- 15ml olive oil
- Salt and pepper to taste

INSTRUCTIONS:

1 Sauté onion and garlic in olive oil until softened.

2 Add red lentils, chopped tomatoes, and vegetable broth.

3 Cook until lentils are tender.

4 Blend until smooth.

5 Season with salt and pepper.

6 Serve hot.

8. POTATO AND ROSEMARY SOUP

Warm up with the comforting flavours of potato and rosemary soup. The earthiness of potatoes and the fragrant rosemary make this soup a cosy choice.

Nutritional Information (per serving):
Calories: 150 kcal | Carbohydrates: 30g | Protein: 3g | Fat: 3g

INGREDIENTS:

- 400g potatoes, peeled and diced
- 1 onion, chopped
- 2 cloves garlic, minced
- 5g fresh rosemary leaves
- 1 litre vegetable broth
- 15ml olive oil
- Salt and pepper to taste

INSTRUCTIONS:

1 Sauté onion and garlic in olive oil until softened.

2 Add diced potatoes, fresh rosemary leaves, and vegetable broth.

3 Cook until potatoes are tender.

4 Blend until smooth.

5 Season with salt and pepper.

6 Serve hot.

9. BROCCOLI AND ALMOND SOUP

Indulge in the creamy richness of broccoli and almond soup. The combination of tender broccoli and toasted almonds adds depth to this soup.

Nutritional Information (per serving):
Calories: 180 kcal | Carbohydrates: 20g | Protein: 6g | Fat: 10g

INGREDIENTS:

- 400g broccoli florets
- 50g almonds, toasted and chopped
- 1 onion, chopped
- 2 cloves garlic, minced
- 1 litre vegetable broth
- 15ml olive oil
- Salt and pepper to taste

INSTRUCTIONS:

1 Sauté onion and garlic in olive oil until softened.
2 Add broccoli florets, toasted almonds, and vegetable broth.
3 Cook until broccoli is tender.
4 Blend until smooth.
5 Season with salt and pepper.
6 Serve hot.

10. PUMPKIN AND SAGE SOUP

Embrace the flavours of autumn with pumpkin and sage soup. The rich, velvety texture of pumpkin and the earthy aroma of sage create a delightful combination.

Nutritional Information (per serving):
Calories: 150 kcal | Carbohydrates: 20g | Protein: 3g | Fat: 7g

INGREDIENTS:

- 400g pumpkin, peeled and diced
- 1 onion, chopped
- 2 cloves garlic, minced
- 10g fresh sage leaves
- 1 litre vegetable broth
- 15ml olive oil
- Salt and pepper to taste

INSTRUCTIONS:

1 Sauté onion and garlic in olive oil until softened.

2 Add diced pumpkin, fresh sage leaves, and vegetable broth.

3 Cook until pumpkin is tender.

4 Blend until smooth.

5 Season with salt and pepper.

6 Serve hot.

11. ASPARAGUS AND SPINACH SOUP

Experience the freshness of asparagus and spinach soup. The combination of tender asparagus and vibrant spinach creates a light and nutritious soup.

Nutritional Information (per serving):
Calories: 120 kcal | Carbohydrates: 15g | Protein: 5g | Fat: 5g

INGREDIENTS:

- 400g asparagus spears, trimmed and chopped
- 200g fresh spinach
- 1 onion, chopped
- 2 cloves garlic, minced
- 1 litre vegetable broth
- 15ml olive oil
- Salt and pepper to taste

INSTRUCTIONS:

1 Sauté onion and garlic in olive oil until softened.

2 Add asparagus spears, fresh spinach, and vegetable broth.

3 Cook until asparagus is tender.

4 Blend until smooth.

5 Season with salt and pepper.

6 Serve hot.

12. BUTTERNUT SQUASH AND SAGE SOUP

Warm up with the comforting flavours of butternut squash and sage soup. The natural sweetness of butternut squash and the earthy aroma of sage make this a cosy choice.

Nutritional Information (per serving):
Calories: 160 kcal | Carbohydrates: 30g | Protein: 2g | Fat: 4g

INGREDIENTS:

- 400g butternut squash, peeled and diced
- 1 onion, chopped
- 2 cloves garlic, minced
- 10g fresh sage leaves
- 1 litre vegetable broth
- 15ml olive oil
- Salt and pepper to taste

INSTRUCTIONS:

1 Sauté onion and garlic in olive oil until softened.

2 Add diced butternut squash, fresh sage leaves, and vegetable broth.

3 Cook until butternut squash is tender.

4 Blend until smooth.

5 Season with salt and pepper.

6 Serve hot.

INTERNATIONAL SOUP MAKER RECIPE DISHES

The tapestry of global cuisine is vast and varied, with each culture bringing its unique flavours, techniques, and stories to the culinary table. Among the diverse dishes that the world has to offer, soups stand out as universal comfort food, yet with regional nuances that make each preparation distinct and memorable.

In this chapter, we'll traverse continents and cultures, exploring the rich landscape of international soups. Each recipe offers a passport to a different corner of the world, from the spicy tom yum of Thailand to the hearty minestrone of Italy, or the rejuvenating miso soup of Japan to the aromatic harira from Morocco.

As we journey through these global recipes, the soup maker emerges as the modern traveller's trusty companion. Simplifying traditional techniques without compromising on authenticity, it ensures that the essence of each region's culinary heritage is captured in every bowl.

So, fasten your seatbelts and prepare your taste buds for a whirlwind tour of the world's kitchens. These international soup dishes, with their myriad flavours and stories, promise a culinary voyage that celebrates the shared human love for soul-warming broths and stews.

1. FRENCH ONION SOUP

A classic French Onion Soup with caramelised onions and melted cheese.

Nutritional Information (per serving):
Calories: 280 kcal | Carbohydrates: 25g | Protein: 8g | Fat: 15g

INGREDIENTS:

- 500g onions, thinly sliced
- 30g butter
- 1 litre beef broth
- Salt and pepper to taste
- Baguette slices
- 100g Gruyère cheese, grated

INSTRUCTIONS:

1 Place onions and butter in the soup maker. Use the "sauté" function and cook until caramelised.
2 Add beef broth, salt, and pepper. Close the lid and select the "soup" function.
3 Once done, toast baguette slices and top with grated cheese.
4 Serve hot with the cheesy bread on top.

2. ITALIAN MINESTRONE SOUP

A hearty Italian Minestrone Soup packed with vegetables, pasta, and beans.

Nutritional Information (per serving):
Calories: 220 kcal | Carbohydrates: 40g | Protein: 8g | Fat: 4g

INGREDIENTS:

- 200g pasta (e.g., small shells)
- 400g canned kidney beans, drained
- 2 carrots, diced
- 2 celery stalks, diced
- 1 onion, chopped
- 1 litre vegetable broth
- 400g canned diced tomatoes
- 15ml olive oil
- Salt and pepper to taste

INSTRUCTIONS:

1 Place pasta, kidney beans, carrots, celery, onion, and canned tomatoes in the soup maker.
2 Add vegetable broth, olive oil, salt, and pepper.
3 Select the "soup" function and let it cook until the pasta and vegetables are tender.
4 Serve hot.

3. THAI TOM YUM SOUP

Experience the bold and tangy flavours of Thailand with Tom Yum Soup, featuring shrimp, mushrooms, and lemongrass.

Nutritional Information (per serving):
Calories: 180 kcal | Carbohydrates: 15g | Protein: 15g | Fat: 6g

INGREDIENTS:
- 200g shrimp, peeled and deveined
- 200g mushrooms, sliced
- 2 lemongrass stalks, sliced
- 3 kaffir lime leaves
- 2 cloves garlic, minced
- 1 litre chicken broth
- 30ml fish sauce
- 15ml lime juice
- 5g fresh coriander leaves
- Red chilli flakes (to taste)

INSTRUCTIONS:
1 Place lemongrass, kaffir lime leaves, garlic, and chicken broth in the soup maker.
2 Add shrimp and mushrooms.
3 Select the "soup" function and let it cook until the shrimp turn pink.
4 Stir in fish sauce and lime juice.
5 Garnish with coriander and red chilli flakes.
6 Serve hot.

4. JAPANESE MISO SOUP

Delight in the simplicity of Japanese Miso Soup, featuring tofu, seaweed, and miso paste.

Nutritional Information (per serving):
Calories: 80 kcal | Carbohydrates: 6g | Protein: 5g | Fat: 4g

INGREDIENTS:
- 300g tofu, diced
- 15g seaweed (e.g., wakame)
- 2 tbsps miso paste
- 1 litre dashi (Japanese fish broth)
- Green onions, chopped

INSTRUCTIONS:
1 Place dashi, seaweed, and tofu in the soup maker.
2 Select the "soup" function and let it simmer until the seaweed and tofu are heated through.
3 Dissolve miso paste in a bit of broth and add to the soup.
4 Garnish with chopped green onions.
5 Serve hot.

5. INDIAN MULLIGATAWNY SOUP

Experience the spices of India with Mulligatawny Soup, a hearty lentil and chicken soup with a hint of curry.

Nutritional Information (per serving):
Calories: 250 kcal | Carbohydrates: 20g | Protein: 15g | Fat: 12g

INGREDIENTS:
- 250g chicken breast, diced
- 150g red lentils
- 1 onion, chopped
- 2 cloves garlic, minced
- 1 litre chicken broth
- 15ml olive oil
- 10g curry powder
- Salt and pepper to taste

INSTRUCTIONS:
1. Place onion and garlic in the soup maker with olive oil.
2. Use the "sauté" function and cook until softened.
3. Add diced chicken and cook until browned.
4. Stir in curry powder and red lentils.
5. Pour in chicken broth.
6. Select the "soup" function and let it simmer until lentils are tender.
7. Season with salt and pepper.
8. Serve hot.

6. MEXICAN TORTILLA SOUP

Spice up your meal with Mexican Tortilla Soup, featuring shredded chicken, tortilla strips, and avocado.

Nutritional Information (per serving):
Calories: 260 kcal | Carbohydrates: 20g | Protein: 18g | Fat: 12g

INGREDIENTS:
- 250g chicken breast, shredded
- 50g tortilla strips
- 1 onion, chopped
- 2 cloves garlic, minced
- 1 litre chicken broth
- 2 tomatoes, chopped
- 1 avocado, diced
- 10g fresh coriander leaves
- Lime wedges

INSTRUCTIONS:

1 Place onion and garlic in the soup maker.

2 Use the "sauté" function and cook until softened.

3 Add shredded chicken and cook until browned.

4 Stir in chopped tomatoes and chicken broth.

5 Select the "soup" function and let it simmer until heated through.

6 Garnish with tortilla strips, diced avocado, fresh coriander, and lime wedges.

7 Serve hot.

7. GREEK AVGOLEMONO SOUP

Experience the Mediterranean with Avgolemono Soup, a creamy lemon and chicken soup with orzo.

Nutritional Information (per serving):
Calories: 220 kcal | Carbohydrates: 20g | Protein: 15g | Fat: 8g

INGREDIENTS:

- 200g orzo pasta
- 2 chicken breasts, cooked and shredded
- 2 eggs
- 1 lemon, juiced
- 1 litre chicken broth
- Fresh dill, chopped
- Salt and pepper to taste

INSTRUCTIONS:

1 Place orzo pasta, shredded chicken, and chicken broth in the soup maker.

2 Select the "soup" function and let it cook until the pasta is tender.

3 In a separate bowl, whisk eggs and lemon juice until frothy.

4 Slowly add a ladle of hot broth to the egg mixture, whisking constantly.

5 Pour the egg mixture back into the soup maker, stirring well.

6 Season with salt and pepper.

7 Garnish with fresh chopped dill.

8 Serve hot.

8. CHINESE HOT AND SOUR SOUP

Satisfy your cravings with Chinese Hot and Sour Soup, featuring tofu, mushrooms, and a balance of spicy and tangy flavours.

Nutritional Information (per serving):
Calories: 150 kcal | Carbohydrates: 10g | Protein: 10g | Fat: 8g

INGREDIENTS:

- 200g tofu, diced
- 200g mushrooms, sliced
- 2 tbsps soy sauce
- 2 tbsps rice vinegar
- 1 litre chicken broth
- 2 cloves garlic, minced
- 5g ginger, minced
- 1 egg, beaten
- 10g fresh coriander leaves
- Red chilli flakes (to taste)

INSTRUCTIONS:

1. Place tofu, mushrooms, garlic, ginger, and chicken broth in the soup maker.
2. Add soy sauce and rice vinegar.
3. Select the "soup" function and let it simmer until mushrooms are tender.
4. Slowly drizzle in the beaten egg while stirring constantly.
5. Season with red chilli flakes and garnish with fresh coriander.
6. Serve hot.

9. SPANISH GAZPACHO

Cool down with Spanish Gazpacho, a refreshing tomato-based cold soup with vegetables and herbs.

Nutritional Information (per serving):
Calories: 80 kcal | Carbohydrates: 15g | Protein: 2g | Fat: 2g

INGREDIENTS:

- 500g ripe tomatoes, chopped
- 1 cucumber, chopped
- 1 red bell pepper, chopped
- 1 onion, chopped
- 2 cloves garlic, minced
- 50ml olive oil
- 15ml red wine vinegar
- 1 litre tomato juice
- Salt and pepper to taste
- Fresh basil leaves

INSTRUCTIONS:

1 Place chopped tomatoes, cucumber, red bell pepper, onion, and garlic in the soup maker.

2 Add olive oil, red wine vinegar, and tomato juice.

3 Select the "soup" function and blend until smooth.

4 Season with salt and pepper.

5 Chill in the refrigerator.

6 Garnish with fresh basil leaves.

7 Serve cold.

10. BRAZILIAN FEIJOADA

Experience the flavours of Brazil with Feijoada, a hearty black bean and pork stew.

Nutritional Information (per serving):
Calories: 350 kcal | Carbohydrates: 30g | Protein: 20g | Fat: 15g

INGREDIENTS:

- 400g black beans, cooked
- 200g pork sausage, sliced
- 200g pork shoulder, diced
- 1 onion, chopped
- 2 cloves garlic, minced
- 1 litre chicken broth
- 10g fresh parsley leaves
- 2 bay leaves
- Salt and pepper to taste
- Rice (for serving)

INSTRUCTIONS:

1 Place black beans, pork sausage, pork shoulder, onion, and garlic in the soup maker.

2 Add chicken broth, fresh parsley, bay leaves, salt, and pepper.

3 Select the "soup" function and let it simmer until heated through.

4 Serve with rice.

11. VIETNAMESE PHO

Savour the aromatic flavours of Vietnamese Pho, featuring rice noodles, beef, and a fragrant broth.

Nutritional Information (per serving):
Calories: 300 kcal | Carbohydrates: 30g | Protein: 20g | Fat: 10g

INGREDIENTS:
- 200g rice noodles
- 250g beef slices
- 1 onion, sliced
- 2 cloves garlic, minced
- 1 litre beef broth
- 10g fresh basil leaves
- 10g fresh coriander leaves
- Bean sprouts
- Lime wedges
- Hoisin sauce and Sriracha (to taste)

INSTRUCTIONS:
1 Place rice noodles, beef slices, onion, and garlic in the soup maker.
2 Add beef broth.
3 Select the "soup" function and let it simmer until the beef is cooked and noodles are tender.
4 Serve in bowls, garnish with fresh basil, coriander, bean sprouts, lime wedges, and offer hoisin sauce and Sriracha on the side.
5 Serve hot.

12. RUSSIAN BORSCHT

Warm up with Russian Borscht, a hearty beet soup with beef, vegetables, and sour cream.

Nutritional Information (per serving):
Calories: 280 kcal | Carbohydrates: 30g | Protein: 15g | Fat: 10g

INGREDIENTS:
- 300g beetroot, peeled and diced
- 200g beef stew meat, cubed
- 1 onion, chopped
- 2 cloves garlic, minced
- 1 litre beef broth
- 200g cabbage, shredded
- 2 tbsps red wine vinegar
- Sour cream (for garnish)
- Fresh dill leaves

INSTRUCTIONS:
1 Place beetroot, beef stew meat, onion, and garlic in the soup maker.
2 Add beef broth, shredded cabbage, and red wine vinegar.
3 Select the "soup" function and let it simmer until the beef is tender and beetroot is cooked.
4 Serve hot with a dollop of sour cream and garnish with fresh dill.

HOT AND SPICY

There's something irresistibly compelling about the interplay of heat and taste. It tingles the tongue, invigorates the senses, and creates a crescendo of flavour that resonates long after the last spoonful. Hot and spicy soups are not just meals; they're experiences – a passionate embrace of zest, warmth, and culinary adventure.

In this chapter, we'll dive into the exhilarating world of hot and spicy soups. These bowls promise a journey that straddles the fine line between pleasure and pain, evoking memories of bustling spice markets, sun-drenched chillies drying in the heat, and ancient recipes passed down through generations.

The range of heat in these recipes caters to both the brave and the cautious. And with the modern convenience of soup makers, achieving the perfect balance of heat and flavour becomes an art that's accessible to all.

Join us as we embark on this spicy sojourn, exploring the myriad ways in which heat can be harnessed, celebrated, and savoured. From subtle warmth to blazing intensity, these soups promise a flavourful foray into the dynamic world of spicy culinary delights.

1. FIERY CAJUN GUMBO

Dive into the spicy world of Cajun cuisine with this bold and flavorful gumbo.

Nutritional Information (per serving):
Calories: 280 kcal | Carbohydrates: 25g | Protein: 18g | Fat: 12g

INGREDIENTS:

- 250g andouille sausage, sliced
- 250g chicken thighs, diced
- 1 onion, chopped
- 2 cloves garlic, minced
- 1 green bell pepper, chopped
- 1 red bell pepper, chopped
- 2 celery stalks, chopped
- 200g okra, sliced
- 1 litre chicken broth
- 30ml vegetable oil
- 15g Cajun seasoning (adjust to taste)
- Cooked white rice (for serving)
- Fresh parsley leaves (for garnish)

INSTRUCTIONS:

1 Heat vegetable oil in a soup maker and sauté andouille sausage until browned. Remove and set aside.

2 In the same pot, brown diced chicken thighs. Remove and set aside.

3 Sauté chopped onion, minced garlic, green and red bell peppers, celery, and okra until softened.

4 Return the sausage and chicken to the pot.

5 Sprinkle Cajun seasoning and stir to coat.

6 Add chicken broth.

7 Select the "soup" function and let it simmer until flavours meld.

8 Serve hot over cooked white rice, garnished with fresh parsley leaves.

2. SZECHUAN HOT POT SOUP

Experience the spicy and numbing flavours of Szechuan cuisine with this hot pot soup.

Nutritional Information (per serving):
Calories: 250 kcal | Carbohydrates: 15g | Protein: 20g | Fat: 12g

INGREDIENTS:

- 250g thinly sliced beef
- 150g tofu, cubed
- 100g enoki mushrooms
- 2 cloves garlic, minced
- 1-inch piece ginger, sliced
- 1 red chilli pepper, chopped (adjust to taste)
- 1 litre beef broth
- 30ml Szechuan hot pot sauce (adjust to taste)
- Bok choy leaves
- Fresh coriander leaves (for garnish)

INSTRUCTIONS:

1 Place thinly sliced beef, tofu, enoki mushrooms, minced garlic, ginger, and chopped red chilli pepper in the soup maker.

2 Add beef broth and Szechuan hot pot sauce.

3 Select the "soup" function and let it simmer until beef is cooked and flavours meld.

4 Add bok choy leaves and simmer until wilted.

5 Serve hot, garnished with fresh coriander leaves.

---

3. CREOLE JAMBALAYA SOUP

Take a spicy journey to New Orleans with this Creole-inspired jambalaya soup.

Nutritional Information (per serving):
Calories: 320 kcal | Carbohydrates: 30g | Protein: 20g | Fat: 12g

INGREDIENTS:

- 250g andouille sausage, sliced
- 250g chicken thighs, diced
- 1 onion, chopped
- 1 green bell pepper, chopped
- 2 celery stalks, chopped
- 2 cloves garlic, minced
- 1 red chilli pepper, chopped (adjust to taste)
- 1 litre chicken broth
- 200g diced tomatoes
- 10g Creole seasoning (adjust to taste)
- Cooked rice (for serving)
- Chopped green onions (for garnish)

INSTRUCTIONS:

1 Sauté andouille sausage in a soup maker until browned. Remove and set aside.

2 In the same pot, brown diced chicken thighs. Remove and set aside.

3 Sauté chopped onion, green bell pepper, celery, minced garlic, and red chilli pepper until softened.

4 Return the sausage and chicken to the pot.

5 Sprinkle Creole seasoning and stir to coat.

6 Add chicken broth and diced tomatoes.

7 Select the "soup" function and let it simmer until flavours meld.

8 Serve hot over cooked rice, garnished with chopped green onions.

4. SPICY THAI GREEN CURRY SOUP

Transport your taste buds to Thailand with this aromatic and fiery green curry soup.

Nutritional Information (per serving):
Calories: 280 kcal | Carbohydrates: 15g | Protein: 18g | Fat: 16g

INGREDIENTS:

- 250g chicken breast, sliced
- 400ml coconut milk
- 2 tbsps Thai green curry paste
- 1 litre chicken broth
- 100g bamboo shoots, sliced
- 100g baby corn, sliced
- 50g green beans, chopped
- 1 red chilli pepper, sliced (adjust to taste)
- Fresh basil leaves (for garnish)
- Lime wedges

INSTRUCTIONS:

1 Place sliced chicken breast, coconut milk, Thai green curry paste, and chicken broth in the soup maker.

2 Add bamboo shoots, baby corn, green beans, and red chilli pepper.

3 Select the "soup" function and let it simmer until chicken is cooked and vegetables are tender.

4 Garnish with fresh basil leaves and serve with lime wedges.

5 Serve hot.

5. INDIAN VINDALOO SOUP

Spice up your soup game with this Indian Vindaloo-inspired soup, packed with flavour and heat.

Nutritional Information (per serving):
Calories: 280 kcal | Carbohydrates: 25g | Protein: 14g | Fat: 14g

INGREDIENTS:

- 250g boneless pork shoulder, diced
- 2 potatoes, peeled and diced
- 1 onion, chopped
- 2 cloves garlic, minced
- 2 red chilli peppers, chopped (adjust to taste)
- 1 litre chicken broth
- 15ml white wine vinegar
- 10g vindaloo spice mix (adjust to taste)
- Chopped fresh coriander (for garnish)
- Naan bread (for serving)

INSTRUCTIONS:

1 Sauté diced pork shoulder in a soup maker until browned. Remove and set aside.

2 In the same pot, sauté chopped onion, minced garlic, and chopped red chilli peppers until softened.

3 Return the pork to the pot.

4 Stir in diced potatoes and vindaloo spice mix.

5 Add chicken broth and white wine vinegar.

6 Select the "soup" function and let it simmer until pork is tender.

7 Garnish with chopped fresh coriander and serve with naan bread.

8 Serve hot.

6. MEXICAN DIABLO SOUP

Feel the heat with this fiery Mexican Diablo soup, featuring spicy chorizo and peppers.

Nutritional Information (per serving):
Calories: 320 kcal | Carbohydrates: 20g | Protein: 18g | Fat: 18g

INGREDIENTS:

- 250g spicy chorizo sausage, sliced
- 1 onion, chopped
- 2 cloves garlic, minced
- 2 red chilli peppers, chopped (adjust to taste)
- 2 green chilli peppers, chopped (adjust to taste)
- 1 litre chicken broth
- 2 tomatoes, chopped
- 50g shredded Monterey Jack cheese
- Fresh coriander leaves (for garnish)
- Lime wedges

INSTRUCTIONS:

1 Sauté sliced spicy chorizo sausage in a soup maker until browned. Remove and set aside.

2 In the same pot, sauté chopped onion, minced garlic, and chopped red and green chilli peppers until softened.

3 Return the chorizo to the pot.

4 Stir in chopped tomatoes.

5 Add chicken broth.

6 Select the "soup" function and let it simmer until flavours meld.

7 Serve hot, topped with shredded Monterey Jack cheese, fresh coriander leaves, and lime wedges.

7. KOREAN KIMCHI JJIGAE SOUP

Experience the spicy and tangy flavours of Korea with Kimchi Jjigae soup.

Nutritional Information (per serving):
Calories: 150 kcal | Carbohydrates: 10g | Protein: 8g | Fat: 8g

INGREDIENTS:

- 250g pork belly, sliced
- 200g kimchi, chopped
- 1 onion, chopped
- 2 cloves garlic, minced
- 1 red chilli pepper, chopped (adjust to taste)
- 1 litre beef broth
- 15ml soy sauce
- 5ml sesame oil
- 5g gochugaru (Korean red pepper flakes, adjust to taste)
- 50g tofu, cubed
- Sliced green onions (for garnish)

INSTRUCTIONS:

1 Sauté sliced pork belly in a soup maker until browned. Remove and set aside.
2 In the same pot, sauté chopped kimchi, chopped onion, minced garlic, and chopped red chilli pepper until softened.
3 Return the pork to the pot.
4 Add beef broth, soy sauce, sesame oil, and gochugaru.
5 Select the "soup" function and let it simmer until flavours meld.
6 Add cubed tofu and simmer until heated through.
7 Garnish with sliced green onions.
8 Serve hot.

8. CARIBBEAN SCOTCH BONNET PEPPER SOUP

Get ready for a spicy adventure with this Caribbean-inspired soup featuring the fiery Scotch Bonnet pepper.

Nutritional Information (per serving):
Calories: 180 kcal | Carbohydrates: 15g | Protein: 8g | Fat: 10g

INGREDIENTS:

- 2 Scotch Bonnet peppers, chopped (adjust to taste)
- 250g chicken thighs, diced
- 1 onion, chopped
- 2 cloves garlic, minced
- 200g sweet potato, diced
- 1 litre chicken broth
- 30ml coconut milk
- 10g fresh thyme leaves
- Cooked rice (for serving)
- Lime wedges (for garnish)

INSTRUCTIONS:

1 Sauté chopped Scotch Bonnet peppers in a soup maker until fragrant. Remove and set aside.

2 In the same pot, brown diced chicken thighs. Remove and set aside.

3 Sauté chopped onion, minced garlic, and diced sweet potato until softened.

4 Return the Scotch Bonnet peppers and chicken to the pot.

5 Add chicken broth, coconut milk, and fresh thyme leaves.

6 Select the "soup" function and let it simmer until flavours meld.

7 Serve hot over cooked rice, garnished with lime wedges.

9. ETHIOPIAN DORO WAT SOUP

Explore the rich and spicy flavours of Ethiopia with this Doro Wat-inspired soup.

Nutritional Information (per serving):
Calories: 280 kcal | Carbohydrates: 20g | Protein: 15g | Fat: 15g

INGREDIENTS:

- 250g chicken drumsticks
- 1 onion, chopped
- 2 cloves garlic, minced
- 2 red chilli peppers, chopped (adjust to taste)
- 2 tbsps berbere spice mix (adjust to taste)
- 1 litre chicken broth
- 50g injera (Ethiopian flatbread)
- Fresh coriander leaves (for garnish)

INSTRUCTIONS:

1 Sauté chicken drumsticks in a soup maker until browned. Remove and set aside.

2 In the same pot, sauté chopped onion, minced garlic, and chopped red chilli peppers until softened.

3 Stir in berbere spice mix.

4 Return the chicken to the pot.

5 Add chicken broth and simmer until chicken is cooked and flavours meld.

6 Serve hot with torn pieces of injera and garnished with fresh coriander leaves.

10. PERUVIAN AJI DE GALLINA SOUP

Spice up your day with the flavours of Peru in this Aji de Gallina-inspired soup.

Nutritional Information (per serving):
Calories: 280 kcal | Carbohydrates: 20g | Protein: 15g | Fat: 15g

INGREDIENTS:

- 250g shredded chicken breast
- 1 onion, chopped
- 2 cloves garlic, minced
- 2 yellow chilli peppers, chopped (adjust to taste)
- 1 litre chicken broth
- 100g roasted peanuts, ground
- 50ml evaporated milk
- Sliced boiled eggs (for garnish)
- Sliced black olives (for garnish)

INSTRUCTIONS:

1 Sauté shredded chicken breast in a soup maker until browned. Remove and set aside.
2 In the same pot, sauté chopped onion, minced garlic, and chopped yellow chilli peppers until softened.
3 Return the chicken to the pot.
4 Add chicken broth, ground roasted peanuts, and evaporated milk.
5 Select the "soup" function and let it simmer until flavours meld.
6 Serve hot, garnished with sliced boiled eggs and sliced black olives.

11. SOUTHERN CAJUN SEAFOOD GUMBO

Take a trip to the deep South with this spicy and hearty seafood gumbo.

Nutritional Information (per serving):
Calories: 320 kcal | Carbohydrates: 25g | Protein: 20g | Fat: 15g

INGREDIENTS:

- 200g shrimp, peeled and deveined
- 200g crabmeat
- 200g okra, sliced
- 1 onion, chopped
- 2 cloves garlic, minced
- 1 green bell pepper, chopped
- 1 red bell pepper, chopped
- 1 litre chicken broth
- 30ml vegetable oil
- 15g Cajun seasoning (adjust to taste)
- Cooked white rice (for serving)
- Sliced green onions (for garnish)

INSTRUCTIONS:

1 Heat vegetable oil in a soup maker and sauté okra until it's no longer slimy. Remove and set aside.

2 In the same pot, sauté chopped onion, minced garlic, green and red bell peppers until softened.

3 Stir in Cajun seasoning.

4 Return the okra to the pot.

5 Add chicken broth.

6 Select the "soup" function and let it simmer until flavours meld.

7 Serve hot over cooked white rice, garnished with sliced green onions.

12. INDIAN BHUT JOLOKIA SOUP

Brace yourself for the heat of the world's spiciest pepper, Bhut Jolokia, in this Indian-inspired soup.

Nutritional Information (per serving):
Calories: 200 kcal | Carbohydrates: 15g | Protein: 10g | Fat: 12g

INGREDIENTS:

- 1 Bhut Jolokia pepper (Ghost Pepper), chopped (adjust to taste)
- 250g boneless chicken thighs, diced
- 1 onion, chopped
- 2 cloves garlic, minced
- 1-inch piece ginger, minced
- 1 red chilli pepper, chopped (adjust to taste)
- 1 litre chicken broth
- 30ml coconut oil
- 5g ground turmeric
- Chopped fresh coriander (for garnish)
- Lime wedges

INSTRUCTIONS:

1 Sauté Bhut Jolokia pepper in coconut oil in a soup maker until fragrant. Remove and set aside.

2 In the same pot, sauté chopped onion, minced garlic, minced ginger, and chopped red chilli pepper until softened.

3 Stir in ground turmeric.

4 Return the Bhut Jolokia pepper to the pot.

5 Add chicken broth.

6 Select the "soup" function and let it simmer until flavours meld.

7 Serve hot, garnished with chopped fresh coriander and lime wedges.

13. THAI SPICY SHRIMP TOM YUM SOUP

Experience the bold and fiery flavours of Thailand with this classic Tom Yum soup.

Nutritional Information (per serving):
Calories: 150 kcal | Carbohydrates: 10g | Protein: 12g | Fat: 7g

INGREDIENTS:

- 200g shrimp, peeled and deveined
- 2 lemongrass stalks, smashed
- 2 kaffir lime leaves
- 2 slices galangal (or ginger)
- 2 cloves garlic, minced
- 1 red chilli pepper, sliced (adjust to taste)
- 1 litre chicken broth
- 15ml fish sauce
- 10ml lime juice
- Fresh coriander leaves (for garnish)
- Sliced red chilli peppers (for garnish)

INSTRUCTIONS:

1 Place shrimp, lemongrass stalks, kaffir lime leaves, galangal, minced garlic, and red chilli pepper in the soup maker.
2 Add chicken broth, fish sauce, and lime juice.
3 Select the "soup" function and let it simmer until shrimp are pink and flavours meld.
4 Garnish with fresh coriander leaves and sliced red chilli peppers.
5 Serve hot.

14. KOREAN SPICY TOFU AND KIMCHI SOUP (KIMCHI JJIGAE)

Warm your soul with this spicy Korean tofu and kimchi stew.

Nutritional Information (per serving):
Calories: 180 kcal | Carbohydrates: 15g | Protein: 10g | Fat: 8g

INGREDIENTS:

- 200g tofu, cubed
- 200g kimchi, chopped
- 1 onion, chopped
- 2 cloves garlic, minced
- 1 red chilli pepper, chopped (adjust to taste)
- 1 litre vegetable broth
- 15ml soy sauce
- 5ml sesame oil
- 5g gochugaru (Korean red pepper flakes, adjust to taste)
- Sliced green onions (for garnish)
- Cooked white rice (for serving)

INSTRUCTIONS:

1 Place tofu, chopped kimchi, chopped onion, minced garlic, and chopped red chilli pepper in the soup maker.

2 Add vegetable broth, soy sauce, sesame oil, and gochugaru.

3 Select the "soup" function and let it simmer until tofu is heated through and flavours meld.

4 Garnish with sliced green onions.

5 Serve hot with cooked white rice.

15. MEXICAN SPICY POZOLE SOUP

Discover the spice of Mexico with this hearty and spicy pozole soup.

Nutritional Information (per serving):
Calories: 300 kcal | Carbohydrates: 25g | Protein: 18g | Fat: 15g

INGREDIENTS:

- 250g pork shoulder, diced
- 1 onion, chopped
- 2 cloves garlic, minced
- 2 red chilli peppers, chopped (adjust to taste)
- 1 litre chicken broth
- 200g hominy (canned or dried and soaked)
- 5g dried oregano
- Chopped fresh coriander (for garnish)
- Lime wedges

INSTRUCTIONS:

1 Sauté diced pork shoulder in a soup maker until browned. Remove and set aside.

2 In the same pot, sauté chopped onion, minced garlic, and chopped red chilli peppers until softened.

3 Return the pork to the pot.

4 Add chicken broth, hominy, and dried oregano.

5 Select the "soup" function and let it simmer until pork is tender and flavours meld.

6 Serve hot, garnished with chopped fresh coriander and lime wedges.

16. JAMAICAN SPICY JERK CHICKEN SOUP

Take a flavorful journey to Jamaica with this spicy jerk chicken soup.

Nutritional Information (per serving):
Calories: 280 kcal | Carbohydrates: 20g | Protein: 15g | Fat: 15g

INGREDIENTS:
- 250g jerk-seasoned chicken thighs, diced
- 1 onion, chopped
- 2 cloves garlic, minced
- 1 Scotch Bonnet pepper, chopped (adjust to taste)
- 1 litre chicken broth
- 200g yam, peeled and diced
- 100g callaloo leaves (substitute spinach if unavailable)
- Fresh thyme leaves (for garnish)
- Cooked rice (for serving)

INSTRUCTIONS:
1. Sauté jerk-seasoned chicken thighs in a soup maker until browned. Remove and set aside.
2. In the same pot, sauté chopped onion, minced garlic, and chopped Scotch Bonnet pepper until softened.
3. Return the chicken to the pot.
4. Stir in diced yam.
5. Add chicken broth and simmer until yam is tender.
6. Add callaloo leaves and simmer until wilted.
7. Serve hot over cooked rice, garnished with fresh thyme leaves.

17. SICHUAN SPICY MAPO TOFU SOUP

Delight in the fiery flavours of Sichuan cuisine with this spicy Mapo Tofu soup.

Nutritional Information (per serving):
Calories: 220 kcal | Carbohydrates: 15g | Protein: 12g | Fat: 15g

INGREDIENTS:
- 200g tofu, cubed
- 250g ground pork
- 2 cloves garlic, minced
- 1-inch piece ginger, minced
- 1 red chilli pepper, chopped (adjust to taste)
- 1 litre chicken broth
- 15ml soy sauce
- 5ml Sichuan peppercorn oil
- 5g doubanjiang (spicy bean paste, adjust to taste)
- Sliced green onions (for garnish)
- Cooked white rice (for serving)

INSTRUCTIONS:

1 Sauté ground pork in a soup maker until browned. Remove and set aside.
2 In the same pot, sauté minced garlic, minced ginger, and chopped red chilli pepper until fragrant.
3 Return the pork to the pot.
4 Stir in soy sauce, Sichuan peppercorn oil, and doubanjiang.
5 Add chicken broth and tofu.
6 Select the "soup" function and let it simmer until tofu is heated through.
7 Serve hot with sliced green onions and cooked white rice.

18. MOROCCAN HARIRA SOUP

Experience the rich and spicy flavours of Morocco with this hearty Harira soup.

Nutritional Information (per serving):
Calories: 280 kcal | Carbohydrates: 20g | Protein: 15g | Fat: 15g

INGREDIENTS:

- 250g lamb shoulder, diced
- 1 onion, chopped
- 2 cloves garlic, minced
- 2 red chilli peppers, chopped (adjust to taste)
- 1 litre chicken broth
- 100g red lentils
- 30g fresh coriander leaves
- 5g ground cumin
- Slices of lemon (for garnish)

INSTRUCTIONS:

1 Sauté diced lamb shoulder in a soup maker until browned. Remove and set aside.
2 In the same pot, sauté chopped onion, minced garlic, and chopped red chilli peppers until softened.
3 Return the lamb to the pot.
4 Stir in red lentils and ground cumin.
5 Add chicken broth.
6 Select the "soup" function and let it simmer until lentils are tender.
7 Garnish with fresh coriander leaves and slices of lemon.
8 Serve hot.

19. INDIAN SPICY PANEER TIKKA MASALA SOUP

Enjoy the flavours of India with this spicy and creamy Paneer Tikka Masala soup.

Nutritional Information (per serving):
Calories: 250 kcal | Carbohydrates: 20g | Protein: 12g | Fat: 15g

INGREDIENTS:

- 250g paneer cheese, cubed
- 1 onion, chopped
- 2 cloves garlic, minced
- 1 red chilli pepper, chopped (adjust to taste)
- 1-inch piece ginger, minced
- 1 litre vegetable broth
- 100ml tomato puree
- 50ml heavy cream
- 5g garam masala
- Fresh coriander leaves (for garnish)
- Naan bread (for serving)

INSTRUCTIONS:

1 Sauté cubed paneer cheese in a soup maker until browned. Remove and set aside.
2 In the same pot, sauté chopped onion, minced garlic, chopped red chilli pepper, and minced ginger until softened.
3 Return the paneer to the pot.
4 Stir in tomato puree and garam masala.
5 Add vegetable broth and heavy cream.
6 Select the "soup" function and let it simmer until flavours meld.
7 Garnish with fresh coriander leaves and serve with naan bread.
8 Serve hot.

20. LOUISIANA SPICY SHRIMP ETOUFFEE SOUP

Take your taste buds to the bayou with this spicy and flavorful shrimp étouffée soup.

Nutritional Information (per serving):
Calories: 280 kcal | Carbohydrates: 25g | Protein: 20g | Fat: 12g

INGREDIENTS:

- 200g shrimp, peeled and deveined
- 1 onion, chopped
- 2 cloves garlic, minced
- 1 green bell pepper, chopped
- 1 red bell pepper, chopped
- 2 celery stalks, chopped
- 1 litre chicken broth
- 30ml vegetable oil
- 15g Cajun seasoning (adjust to taste)
- Cooked white rice (for serving)
- Fresh parsley leaves (for garnish)

INSTRUCTIONS:

1 Heat vegetable oil in a soup maker and sauté chopped onion, minced garlic, chopped green and red bell peppers, and chopped celery until softened.

2 Stir in Cajun seasoning.

3 Add chicken broth and shrimp.

4 Select the "soup" function and let it simmer until shrimp are pink and flavours meld.

5 Serve hot over cooked white rice, garnished with fresh parsley leaves.

21. THAI SPICY RED CURRY CHICKEN SOUP

Embark on a spicy Thai adventure with this vibrant red curry chicken soup.

Nutritional Information (per serving):
Calories: 280 kcal | Carbohydrates: 15g | Protein: 18g | Fat: 15g

INGREDIENTS:

- 250g chicken breast, sliced
- 400ml coconut milk
- 2 tbsps Thai red curry paste
- 1 litre chicken broth
- 100g bamboo shoots, sliced
- 100g red bell pepper, sliced
- 5g fresh basil leaves
- 1 red chilli pepper, sliced (adjust to taste)
- Lime wedges

INSTRUCTIONS:

1 Place sliced chicken breast, coconut milk, Thai red curry paste, and chicken broth in the soup maker.

2 Add bamboo shoots, sliced red bell pepper, and fresh basil leaves.

3 Select the "soup" function and let it simmer until chicken is cooked and vegetables are tender.

4 Garnish with sliced red chilli pepper and serve with lime wedges.

5 Serve hot.

22. MEXICAN SPICY CHICKEN TORTILLA SOUP

Savour the flavours of Mexico with this spicy and comforting chicken tortilla soup.

Nutritional Information (per serving):
Calories: 250 kcal | Carbohydrates: 20g | Protein: 15g | Fat: 15g

INGREDIENTS:

- 250g chicken breast, diced
- 1 onion, chopped
- 2 cloves garlic, minced
- 1 red chilli pepper, chopped (adjust to taste)
- 1 litre chicken broth
- 400g diced tomatoes
- 30g tortilla chips, crushed
- 30g shredded cheddar cheese
- Fresh coriander leaves (for garnish)
- Lime wedges

INSTRUCTIONS:

1. Sauté diced chicken breast in a soup maker until browned. Remove and set aside.
2. In the same pot, sauté chopped onion, minced garlic, and chopped red chilli pepper until softened.
3. Return the chicken to the pot.
4. Stir in diced tomatoes and chicken broth.
5. Select the "soup" function and let it simmer until flavours meld.
6. Serve hot, garnished with crushed tortilla chips, shredded cheddar cheese, fresh coriander leaves, and lime wedges.

23. INDONESIAN SPICY RENDANG SOUP

Discover the bold flavours of Indonesia with this spicy and aromatic Rendang soup.

Nutritional Information (per serving):
Calories: 280 kcal | Carbohydrates: 15g | Protein: 18g | Fat: 15g

INGREDIENTS:

- 250g beef stew meat, sliced
- 1 onion, chopped
- 2 cloves garlic, minced
- 1-inch piece ginger, minced
- 1 red chilli pepper, chopped (adjust to taste)
- 1 litre beef broth
- 400ml coconut milk
- 5g Rendang spice mix (adjust to taste)
- Fresh basil leaves (for garnish)
- Cooked rice (for serving)

INSTRUCTIONS:

1 Sauté sliced beef stew meat in a soup maker until browned. Remove and set aside.

2 In the same pot, sauté chopped onion, minced garlic, minced ginger, and chopped red chilli pepper until softened.

3 Return the beef to the pot.

4 Stir in Rendang spice mix.

5 Add beef broth and coconut milk.

6 Select the "soup" function and let it simmer until beef is tender and flavours meld.

7 Garnish with fresh basil leaves and serve with cooked rice.

8 Serve hot.

24. TURKISH SPICY LENTIL AND BULGUR SOUP (EZO GELIN ÇORBASI)

Experience the comforting flavours of Turkey with this spicy lentil and bulgur soup.

Nutritional Information (per serving):
Calories: 200 kcal | Carbohydrates: 20g | Protein: 10g | Fat: 8g

INGREDIENTS:

- 100g red lentils
- 50g fine bulgur
- 1 onion, chopped
- 2 cloves garlic, minced
- 1 red chilli pepper, chopped (adjust to taste)
- 1 litre vegetable broth
- 15ml tomato paste
- 5g dried mint
- 30ml olive oil
- Slices of lemon (for garnish)

INSTRUCTIONS:

1 Sauté chopped onion, minced garlic, and chopped red chilli pepper in olive oil in a soup maker until softened.

2 Stir in tomato paste.

3 Add red lentils, fine bulgur, and vegetable broth.

4 Select the "soup" function and let it simmer until lentils and bulgur are tender.

5 Garnish with dried mint and slices of lemon.

6 Serve hot.

25. CARIBBEAN SPICY GOAT CURRY SOUP

Taste the Caribbean with this spicy and aromatic goat curry soup.

Nutritional Information (per serving):
Calories: 280 kcal | Carbohydrates: 20g | Protein: 15g | Fat: 15g

INGREDIENTS:

- 250g goat meat, diced
- 1 onion, chopped
- 2 cloves garlic, minced
- 1 Scotch Bonnet pepper, chopped (adjust to taste)
- 1-inch piece ginger, minced
- 1 litre chicken broth
- 10g curry powder (adjust to taste)
- 100g diced potatoes
- Fresh thyme leaves (for garnish)
- Slices of lime (for garnish)
- Cooked rice (for serving)

INSTRUCTIONS:

1 Sauté diced goat meat in a soup maker until browned. Remove and set aside.
2 In the same pot, sauté chopped onion, minced garlic, chopped Scotch Bonnet pepper, and minced ginger until softened.
3 Return the goat meat to the pot.
4 Stir in curry powder.
5 Add chicken broth and diced potatoes.
6 Select the "soup" function and let it simmer until goat meat is tender.
7 Garnish with fresh thyme leaves and slices of lime.
8 Serve hot over cooked rice.

26. THAI SPICY PINEAPPLE CURRY SOUP

Experience the sweet and spicy flavours of Thailand with this pineapple curry soup.

Nutritional Information (per serving):
Calories: 250 kcal | Carbohydrates: 20g | Protein: 12g | Fat: 15g

INGREDIENTS:

- 250g chicken breast, sliced
- 400ml coconut milk
- 2 tbsps Thai yellow curry paste
- 250ml diced pineapple
- 1 litre chicken broth
- 50g baby corn, sliced
- Fresh basil leaves (for garnish)
- Lime wedges

INSTRUCTIONS:

1 Place sliced chicken breast, coconut milk, Thai yellow curry paste, diced pineapple, and chicken broth in the soup maker.

2 Add sliced baby corn.

3 Select the "soup" function and let it simmer until chicken is cooked and baby corn is tender.

4 Garnish with fresh basil leaves and serve with lime wedges.

5 Serve hot.

27. CHINESE HOT AND SOUR SOUP

Warm up with this classic Chinese hot and sour soup, packed with spicy and tangy flavours.

Nutritional Information (per serving):
Calories: 180 kcal | Carbohydrates: 15g | Protein: 10g | Fat: 8g

INGREDIENTS:

- 100g tofu, cubed
- 100g shiitake mushrooms, sliced
- 2 wood ear mushrooms, soaked and sliced
- 2 slices ginger
- 2 cloves garlic, minced
- 1 red chilli pepper, chopped (adjust to taste)
- 1 litre chicken broth
- 30ml rice vinegar
- 15ml soy sauce
- 5ml sesame oil
- Sliced green onions (for garnish)
- Crispy fried wonton strips (for garnish)

INSTRUCTIONS:

1 Place cubed tofu, sliced shiitake mushrooms, soaked and sliced wood ear mushrooms, ginger slices, minced garlic, and chopped red chilli pepper in the soup maker.

2 Add chicken broth, rice vinegar, soy sauce, and sesame oil.

3 Select the "soup" function and let it simmer until flavours meld.

4 Garnish with sliced green onions and crispy fried wonton strips.

5 Serve hot.

28. ITALIAN SPICY SAUSAGE AND PEPPER SOUP

Enjoy the bold flavours of Italy with this spicy sausage and pepper soup.

Nutritional Information (per serving):
Calories: 320 kcal | Carbohydrates: 25g | Protein: 18g | Fat: 15g

INGREDIENTS:

- 250g spicy Italian sausage, sliced
- 1 onion, chopped
- 2 cloves garlic, minced
- 1 red chilli pepper, chopped (adjust to taste)
- 1 litre chicken broth
- 400g diced tomatoes
- 1 red bell pepper, chopped
- 1 yellow bell pepper, chopped
- 1 green bell pepper, chopped
- Fresh basil leaves (for garnish)
- Grated Parmesan cheese (for garnish)

INSTRUCTIONS:

1 Sauté sliced spicy Italian sausage in a soup maker until browned. Remove and set aside.
2 In the same pot, sauté chopped onion, minced garlic, and chopped red chilli pepper until softened.
3 Return the sausage to the pot.
4 Stir in diced tomatoes, chicken broth, and chopped red, yellow, and green bell peppers.
5 Select the "soup" function and let it simmer until flavours meld.
6 Garnish with fresh basil leaves and grated Parmesan cheese.
7 Serve hot.

29. SPANISH SPICY CHORIZO AND CHICKPEA SOUP

Savour the flavours of Spain with this spicy chorizo and chickpea soup.

Nutritional Information (per serving):
Calories: 280 kcal | Carbohydrates: 20g | Protein: 15g | Fat: 15g

INGREDIENTS:

- 250g spicy chorizo sausage, sliced
- 1 onion, chopped
- 2 cloves garlic, minced
- 1 red chilli pepper, chopped (adjust to taste)
- 1 litre chicken broth
- 200g canned chickpeas, drained and rinsed
- 100g diced tomatoes
- Smoked paprika (for garnish)
- Fresh parsley leaves (for garnish)

INSTRUCTIONS:

1 Sauté sliced spicy chorizo sausage in a soup maker until browned. Remove and set aside.

2 In the same pot, sauté chopped onion, minced garlic, and chopped red chilli pepper until softened.

3 Return the chorizo to the pot.

4 Stir in diced tomatoes, chicken broth, and canned chickpeas.

5 Select the "soup" function and let it simmer until flavours meld.

6 Garnish with smoked paprika and fresh parsley leaves.

7 Serve hot.

30. THAI SPICY SEAFOOD TOM KHA SOUP

Indulge in the vibrant flavours of Thailand with this spicy seafood Tom Kha soup.

Nutritional Information (per serving):
Calories: 280 kcal | Carbohydrates: 15g | Protein: 18g | Fat: 15g

INGREDIENTS:

- 200g shrimp, peeled and deveined
- 200g squid, sliced into rings
- 400ml coconut milk
- 2 slices galangal (or ginger)
- 2 kaffir lime leaves
- 2 lemongrass stalks, smashed
- 1 red chilli pepper, sliced (adjust to taste)
- 1 litre chicken broth
- 15ml fish sauce
- 10ml lime juice
- Fresh coriander leaves (for garnish)
- Sliced red chilli peppers (for garnish)

INSTRUCTIONS:

1 Place peeled and deveined shrimp, sliced squid, coconut milk, galangal slices, kaffir lime leaves, lemongrass stalks, sliced red chilli pepper, chicken broth, fish sauce, and lime juice in the soup maker.

2 Select the "soup" function and let it simmer until seafood is cooked and flavours meld.

3 Garnish with fresh coriander leaves and sliced red chilli peppers.

4 Serve hot.

FUNKY AND "OUT THERE" SOUP RECIPES

The world of soup is as vast as it is varied, and while many of us find solace in the familiar, there lies an adventurous realm beckoning the bold. This is the world of the funky, the unconventional, and the utterly „out there." A place where traditional boundaries are blurred, and culinary norms are playfully, often audaciously, challenged.

In this chapter, we'll voyage into the unexpected, unearthing recipes that challenge conventions and tantalise the senses in ways you might never have imagined. These aren't just soups; they're conversation starters, fusions of ingredients that might raise eyebrows, yet undoubtedly intrigue the palate.

From whimsical combinations to avant-garde techniques, these „out there" recipes turn the act of soup-making into an exciting experimental journey. With the help of modern soup makers, even the most audacious of these recipes become accessible, allowing you to take culinary risks with confidence.

So, if you're ready to shake things up, to embark on a gastronomic adventure that promises the unexpected at every turn, then delve into this chapter with an open mind and an eager palate. Here, we celebrate the weird, the wonderful, and the wondrously funky in the world of soups.

1. JAPANESE MISO PUMPKIN SOUP

A twist on traditional miso soup with the sweet addition of pumpkin.

Nutritional Information (per serving):
Calories: 150 kcal | Carbohydrates: 12g | Protein: 5g | Fat: 8g

INGREDIENTS:

- 300g pumpkin, cubed
- 2 tbsps miso paste
- 1 litre vegetable broth
- 10g seaweed (kombu or wakame)
- 1 green onion, thinly sliced (for garnish)
- Sesame seeds (for garnish)

INSTRUCTIONS:

1 Place cubed pumpkin and seaweed in the soup maker.

2 Add vegetable broth and let it simmer until the pumpkin is tender.

3 Dissolve miso paste in a small amount of warm water and stir it into the soup.

4 Serve hot, garnished with thinly sliced green onion and sesame seeds.

2. ITALIAN PESTO AND WHITE BEAN SOUP

A flavorful Italian-inspired soup with the richness of pesto and creamy white beans.

Nutritional Information (per serving):
Calories: 220 kcal | Carbohydrates: 20g | Protein: 8g | Fat: 12g

INGREDIENTS:

- 200g cannellini beans, cooked and drained
- 2 tbsps pesto sauce
- 1 litre vegetable broth
- 100g baby spinach
- Grated Parmesan cheese (for garnish)

INSTRUCTIONS:

1 Place cooked cannellini beans in the soup maker.

2 Add vegetable broth and let it simmer until the beans are heated through.

3 Stir in pesto sauce.

4 Add baby spinach and let it wilt.

5 Serve hot, garnished with grated Parmesan cheese.

3. GREEK LEMON AVGOLEMONO SOUP

Experience the zesty flavours of Greece with this lemony chicken and rice soup.

Nutritional Information (per serving):
Calories: 200 kcal | Carbohydrates: 15g | Protein: 12g | Fat: 10g

INGREDIENTS:

- 250g chicken breast, cooked and shredded
- 100g rice
- 2 eggs
- Juice of 2 lemons
- 1 litre chicken broth
- Fresh dill (for garnish)

INSTRUCTIONS:

1. Place shredded chicken and rice in the soup maker.
2. Add chicken broth and let it simmer until the rice is tender.
3. In a separate bowl, beat eggs and lemon juice until frothy.
4. Gradually whisk the egg-lemon mixture into the soup.
5. Serve hot, garnished with fresh dill.

4. MEXICAN CHOCOLATE CHILI SOUP

A surprising combination of chocolate and chilli for a unique Mexican-inspired soup.

Nutritional Information (per serving):
Calories: 180 kcal | Carbohydrates: 20g | Protein: 8g | Fat: 8g

INGREDIENTS:

- 400g black beans, cooked and drained
- 30g unsweetened cocoa powder
- 1 red chilli pepper, chopped (adjust to taste)
- 1 litre vegetable broth
- Sour cream (for garnish)
- Chopped coriander (for garnish)

INSTRUCTIONS:

1. Place cooked black beans and chopped red chilli pepper in the soup maker.
2. Add vegetable broth and let it simmer until the beans are heated through.
3. Stir in unsweetened cocoa powder.
4. Serve hot, garnished with a dollop of sour cream and chopped coriander.

5. THAI GREEN CURRY NOODLE SOUP

A fusion of Thai green curry and noodle soup for a flavorful and spicy delight.

Nutritional Information (per serving):
Calories: 280 kcal | Carbohydrates: 25g | Protein: 10g | Fat: 15g

INGREDIENTS:

- 200g rice noodles
- 2 tbsps Thai green curry paste
- 400ml coconut milk
- 1 litre vegetable broth
- 100g broccoli florets
- Fresh basil leaves (for garnish)
- Lime wedges

INSTRUCTIONS:

1. Cook rice noodles according to package Instructions and set aside.
2. Place Thai green curry paste and coconut milk in the soup maker.
3. Add vegetable broth and let it simmer.
4. Add broccoli florets and let them cook until tender.
5. Serve hot over cooked rice noodles, garnished with fresh basil leaves and lime wedges.

6. INDIAN MASALA CHAI SOUP

A warm and comforting soup with the aromatic spices of Indian masala chai.

Nutritional Information (per serving):
Calories: 120 kcal | Carbohydrates: 15g | Protein: 5g | Fat: 5g

INGREDIENTS:

- 500ml milk
- 2 black tea bags
- 1 cinnamon stick
- 4 cloves
- 4 cardamom pods
- 1-inch piece ginger, sliced
- 1 tbsp honey (or adjust to taste)
- Saffron strands (for garnish)

INSTRUCTIONS:

1. Heat milk in the soup maker until it's almost boiling.
2. Add black tea bags, cinnamon stick, cloves, cardamom pods, and sliced ginger.
3. Let it steep for a few minutes, then remove the tea bags and spices.
4. Stir in honey.
5. Serve hot, garnished with saffron strands.

7. VIETNAMESE PHO-INSPIRED SOUP

A twist on classic Vietnamese pho with the addition of exotic mushrooms.

Nutritional Information (per serving):
Calories: 150 kcal | Carbohydrates: 20g | Protein: 8g | Fat: 6g

INGREDIENTS:

- 100g exotic mushrooms (shiitake, oyster, etc.), sliced
- 200g rice noodles
- 1 litre beef broth
- Fresh coriander leaves (for garnish)
- Bean sprouts (for garnish)
- Hoisin sauce and Sriracha (for serving)

INSTRUCTIONS:

1 Place sliced exotic mushrooms in the soup maker.
2 Add beef broth and let it simmer until the mushrooms are tender.
3 Cook rice noodles according to package instructions and set aside.
4 Serve hot with cooked rice noodles, garnished with fresh coriander leaves and bean sprouts. Provide hoisin sauce and Sriracha for added flavour.

8. MEXICAN STREET CORN SOUP

Experience the flavours of Mexican street corn in a comforting soup.

Nutritional Information (per serving):
Calories: 180 kcal | Carbohydrates: 20g | Protein: 5g | Fat: 10g

INGREDIENTS:

- 500ml corn kernels (fresh or frozen)
- 1 red chilli pepper, chopped (adjust to taste)
- 2 tbsps mayonnaise
- Juice of 1 lime
- 1 litre vegetable broth
- Crumbled cotija cheese (for garnish)
- Chopped fresh coriander (for garnish)

INSTRUCTIONS:

1 Place corn kernels and chopped red chilli pepper in the soup maker.
2 Add vegetable broth and let it simmer until corn is tender.
3 Stir in mayonnaise and lime juice.
4 Serve hot, garnished with crumbled cotija cheese and chopped fresh coriander.

9. SPANISH GAZPACHO VERDE

A refreshing twist on Spanish gazpacho with the addition of green vegetables.

Nutritional Information (per serving):
Calories: 120 kcal | Carbohydrates: 15g | Protein: 2g | Fat: 6g

INGREDIENTS:

- 300g cucumber, chopped
- 200g green bell pepper, chopped
- 100g fresh spinach
- 2 cloves garlic, minced
- 2 tbsps olive oil
- 15ml white wine vinegar
- 1 litre vegetable broth
- Sliced green onions (for garnish)

INSTRUCTIONS:

1 Place chopped cucumber, green bell pepper, fresh spinach, and minced garlic in the soup maker.

2 Add vegetable broth and let it simmer until the vegetables are tender.

3 Stir in olive oil and white wine vinegar.

4 Serve cold, garnished with sliced green onions.

10. THAI MANGO STICKY RICE SOUP

A sweet and creamy dessert soup inspired by Thai mango sticky rice.

Nutritional Information (per serving):
Calories: 250 kcal | Carbohydrates: 50g | Protein: 2g | Fat: 5g

INGREDIENTS:

- 200g glutinous rice, cooked and cooled
- 1 ripe mango, diced
- 400ml coconut milk
- 50g palm sugar (or adjust to taste)
- Toasted sesame seeds (for garnish)

INSTRUCTIONS:

1 Place cooked and cooled glutinous rice in the soup maker.

2 Add coconut milk and palm sugar.

3 Let it simmer until heated through.

4 Serve hot or cold, garnished with diced ripe mango and toasted sesame seeds.

11. JAPANESE MATCHA GREEN TEA SOUP

A unique and soothing Japanese-inspired soup featuring the earthy flavours of matcha green tea.

Nutritional Information (per serving):
Calories: 80 kcal | Carbohydrates: 15g | Protein: 2g | Fat: 2g

INGREDIENTS:

- 2 tsps matcha green tea powder
- 400ml milk (dairy or plant-based)
- 30g honey (or adjust to taste)
- Matcha green tea ice cream (for garnish)

INSTRUCTIONS:

1. Whisk matcha green tea powder and honey into milk in the soup maker.
2. Heat the mixture until it's just about to boil.
3. Serve hot or cold, garnished with a scoop of matcha green tea ice cream.

12. INDIAN SPICY CHAI-SPICED SOUP

Warm up with the aromatic spices of Indian chai in this unique soup.

Nutritional Information (per serving):
Calories: 150 kcal | Carbohydrates: 20g | Protein: 5g | Fat: 6g

INGREDIENTS:

- 500ml milk
- 2 chai tea bags
- 2 tbsps honey (or adjust to taste)
- 1 cinnamon stick
- 4 cardamom pods
- Saffron strands (for garnish)

INSTRUCTIONS:

1. Heat milk in the soup maker until it's almost boiling.
2. Add chai tea bags, cinnamon stick, cardamom pods, and saffron strands.
3. Let it steep for a few minutes, then remove the tea bags and spices.
4. Stir in honey.
5. Serve hot, garnished with additional saffron strands if desired.

13. MEXICAN SPICY TAMARIND SOUP

A bold and tangy Mexican-inspired soup with the unique flavour of tamarind.

Nutritional Information (per serving):
Calories: 160 kcal | Carbohydrates: 20g | Protein: 5g | Fat: 7g

INGREDIENTS:

- 100g tamarind pulp (soaked in warm water and strained)
- 1 red chilli pepper, chopped (adjust to taste)
- 1 litre vegetable broth
- 100g jicama, peeled and sliced
- Fresh coriander leaves (for garnish)
- Lime wedges

INSTRUCTIONS:

1. Combine soaked tamarind pulp and chopped red chilli pepper in the soup maker.
2. Add vegetable broth and let it simmer.
3. Add sliced jicama and let it cook until tender.
4. Serve hot, garnished with fresh coriander leaves and lime wedges.

14. KOREAN KIMCHI PANCAKE SOUP

A creative Korean-inspired soup featuring kimchi pancakes in a flavorful broth.

Nutritional Information (per serving):
Calories: 180 kcal | Carbohydrates: 20g | Protein: 8g | Fat: 8g

INGREDIENTS:

- 2 kimchi pancakes (store-bought or homemade, sliced into strips)
- 1 green onion, thinly sliced
- 1 litre vegetable broth
- Sesame seeds (for garnish)
- Gochugaru (Korean red pepper flakes, for garnish)

INSTRUCTIONS:

1. Place sliced kimchi pancakes and thinly sliced green onion in the soup maker.
2. Add vegetable broth and let it simmer until the pancakes are heated through.
3. Serve hot, garnished with sesame seeds and a sprinkle of gochugaru for extra heat.

15. THAI SPICY PAPAYA SALAD SOUP

Experience the bold flavours of Thai papaya salad in a refreshing soup form.

Nutritional Information (per serving):
Calories: 140 kcal | Carbohydrates: 20g | Protein: 5g | Fat: 6g

INGREDIENTS:

- 1 green papaya, peeled and shredded
- 1 red chilli pepper, chopped (adjust to taste)
- 2 cloves garlic, minced
- 1 tbsp fish sauce
- 1 tbsp lime juice
- 1 tsp palm sugar (or adjust to taste)
- 1 litre vegetable broth
- Roasted peanuts (for garnish)
- Fresh mint leaves (for garnish)

INSTRUCTIONS:

1 Combine shredded green papaya, chopped red chilli pepper, minced garlic, fish sauce, lime juice, and palm sugar in the soup maker.

2 Add vegetable broth and let it simmer until the papaya is tender.

3 Serve hot, garnished with roasted peanuts and fresh mint leaves.

16. JAPANESE SPICY WASABI SOUP

A spicy and zesty Japanese-inspired soup featuring the bold flavour of wasabi.

Nutritional Information (per serving):
Calories: 100 kcal | Carbohydrates: 15g | Protein: 2g | Fat: 3g

INGREDIENTS:

- 2 tsps wasabi paste (adjust to taste)
- 400ml vegetable broth
- 100g edamame beans (shelled)
- 2 sheets nori seaweed, torn into strips (for garnish)

INSTRUCTIONS:

1 Whisk wasabi paste into vegetable broth in the soup maker.

2 Add shelled edamame beans and let them simmer until heated through.

3 Serve hot, garnished with torn nori seaweed strips.

17. ITALIAN SPICY PESTO AND POTATO SOUP

A flavorful Italian-inspired soup with the richness of pesto and hearty potatoes.

Nutritional Information (per serving):
Calories: 220 kcal | Carbohydrates: 20g | Protein: 8g | Fat: 12g

INGREDIENTS:

- 200g potatoes, peeled and diced
- 2 tbsps pesto sauce
- 1 litre vegetable broth
- Grated Parmesan cheese (for garnish)
- Fresh basil leaves (for garnish)

INSTRUCTIONS:

1. Place diced potatoes in the soup maker.
2. Add vegetable broth and let it simmer until the potatoes are tender.
3. Stir in pesto sauce.
4. Serve hot, garnished with grated Parmesan cheese and fresh basil leaves.

18. THAI TOM YUM COCONUT SOUP

A fusion of Thai tom yum and coconut soup for a spicy and creamy delight.

Nutritional Information (per serving):
Calories: 220 kcal | Carbohydrates: 15g | Protein: 10g | Fat: 15g

INGREDIENTS:

- 200g shrimp, peeled and deveined
- 400ml coconut milk
- 2 tbsps Thai tom yum paste
- 1 red chilli pepper, sliced (adjust to taste)
- 1 litre chicken broth
- Kaffir lime leaves (for garnish)
- Fresh coriander leaves (for garnish)

INSTRUCTIONS:

1. Place peeled and deveined shrimp, coconut milk, Thai tom yum paste, and sliced red chilli pepper in the soup maker.
2. Add chicken broth and let it simmer until the shrimp are cooked.
3. Garnish with kaffir lime leaves and fresh coriander leaves.
4. Serve hot.

19. GREEK SPICY FETA AND OLIVE SOUP

Experience the bold flavours of Greece with this spicy feta and olive soup.

Nutritional Information (per serving):
Calories: 180 kcal | Carbohydrates: 10g | Protein: 8g | Fat: 12g

INGREDIENTS:

- 100g feta cheese, crumbled
- 50g Kalamata olives, pitted and sliced
- 1 red chilli pepper, chopped (adjust to taste)
- 1 litre vegetable broth
- Chopped fresh oregano leaves (for garnish)

INSTRUCTIONS:

1 Place crumbled feta cheese, sliced Kalamata olives, and chopped red chilli pepper in the soup maker.

2 Add vegetable broth and let it simmer until the feta cheese is melted.

3 Serve hot, garnished with chopped fresh oregano leaves.

20. INDIAN SPICY SAMOSA SOUP

Enjoy the flavours of an Indian samosa in a comforting soup.

Nutritional Information (per serving):
Calories: 200 kcal | Carbohydrates: 20g | Protein: 6g | Fat: 10g

INGREDIENTS:

- 2 potato samosas (store-bought or homemade, crumbled)
- 1 onion, chopped
- 2 cloves garlic, minced
- 1 red chilli pepper, chopped (adjust to taste)
- 1 litre vegetable broth
- Chopped fresh coriander leaves (for garnish)
- Tamarind chutney (for serving)

INSTRUCTIONS:

1 Place crumbled potato samosas, chopped onion, minced garlic, and chopped red chilli pepper in the soup maker.

2 Add vegetable broth and let it simmer until heated through.

3 Serve hot, garnished with chopped fresh coriander leaves and a drizzle of tamarind chutney.

GREEN POWER SOUP RECIPES

Amidst the diverse palette of culinary colours, there's one hue that universally resonates with vitality, wellness, and nature itself: green. Beyond its visual appeal, it symbolises a bounty of nutrients, a plethora of flavours, and the pure, rejuvenating essence of Mother Earth.

In this chapter, we'll explore the invigorating realm of Green Power soups. These aren't just soups; they are liquid chlorophyll-filled gems, encapsulating the freshest of greens from leafy kale and spinach to vibrant peas and zesty herbs. Each bowl is a testament to the power of plants and their innate ability to nourish and heal.

With today's innovative soup makers, the vivacity of these ingredients is effortlessly captured, ensuring you extract maximum flavour and nutritional benefits in every spoonful.

Join us on this verdant voyage, where every recipe is a tribute to nature's green bounty. Whether you're seeking detoxification, a boost of energy, or simply a taste of earthy goodness, Green Power soups offer a revitalising embrace that refreshes both body and soul.

1. GREEN GODDESS SPINACH SOUP

A nutrient-packed soup that celebrates the greens with spinach, kale, collard greens, and Swiss chard.

Nutritional Information (per serving):
Calories: 80 kcal | Carbohydrates: 10g | Protein: 4g | Fat: 4g

INGREDIENTS:

- 100g spinach
- 100g kale
- 100g collard greens
- 100g Swiss chard
- 1 onion, chopped
- 2 cloves garlic, minced
- 1 litre vegetable broth
- Fresh parsley leaves (for garnish)

INSTRUCTIONS:

1 Place spinach, kale, collard greens, Swiss chard, chopped onion, and minced garlic in the soup maker.

2 Add vegetable broth and let it simmer until the greens are tender.

3 Serve hot, garnished with fresh parsley leaves.

2. FOUR GREENS POWERHOUSE SOUP

A supercharged soup featuring a quartet of greens: spinach, arugula, watercress, and bok choy.

Nutritional Information (per serving):
Calories: 70 kcal | Carbohydrates: 8g | Protein: 3g | Fat: 3g

INGREDIENTS:

- 100g spinach
- 100g arugula
- 100g watercress
- 100g baby bok choy
- 2 cloves garlic, minced
- 1 leek, chopped
- 1 litre vegetable broth
- Fresh basil leaves (for garnish)

INSTRUCTIONS:

1 Place spinach, arugula, watercress, baby bok choy, minced garlic, and chopped leek in the soup maker.

2 Add vegetable broth and let it simmer until the greens are tender.

3 Serve hot, garnished with fresh basil leaves.

3. MIXED GREENS DETOX SOUP

A detoxifying soup packed with a mix of greens: spinach, Swiss chard, collard greens, and mustard greens.

Nutritional Information (per serving):
Calories: 60 kcal | Carbohydrates: 8g | Protein: 4g | Fat: 2g

INGREDIENTS:

- 100g spinach
- 100g Swiss chard
- 100g collard greens
- 100g mustard greens
- 1 onion, chopped
- 2 cloves garlic, minced
- 1 litre vegetable broth
- Fresh mint leaves (for garnish)

INSTRUCTIONS:

1 Place spinach, Swiss chard, collard greens, mustard greens, chopped onion, and minced garlic in the soup maker.

2 Add vegetable broth and let it simmer until the greens are tender.

3 Serve hot, garnished with fresh mint leaves.

4. LEAFY GREEN SPINACH AND KALE SOUP

A delightful green soup featuring the dynamic duo of spinach and kale along with Swiss chard and arugula.

Nutritional Information (per serving):
Calories: 70 kcal | Carbohydrates: 9g | Protein: 4g | Fat: 3g

INGREDIENTS:

- 100g spinach
- 100g kale
- 100g Swiss chard
- 100g arugula
- 1 onion, chopped
- 2 cloves garlic, minced
- 1 litre vegetable broth
- Fresh coriander leaves (for garnish)

INSTRUCTIONS:

1 Place spinach, kale, Swiss chard, arugula, chopped onion, and minced garlic in the soup maker.

2 Add vegetable broth and let it simmer until the greens are tender.

3 Serve hot, garnished with fresh coriander leaves.

5. FOUR-LEAF CLOVER SOUP

A luck-filled soup featuring the greenery of spinach, collard greens, watercress, and bok choy.

Nutritional Information (per serving):
Calories: 75 kcal | Carbohydrates: 8g | Protein: 4g | Fat: 3g

INGREDIENTS:
- 100g spinach
- 100g collard greens
- 100g watercress
- 100g baby bok choy
- 1 onion, chopped
- 2 cloves garlic, minced
- 1 litre vegetable broth
- Fresh dill leaves (for garnish)

INSTRUCTIONS:
1. Place spinach, collard greens, watercress, baby bok choy, chopped onion, and minced garlic in the soup maker.
2. Add vegetable broth and let it simmer until the greens are tender.
3. Serve hot, garnished with fresh dill leaves.

6. VERDANT SPINACH AND BROCCOLI SOUP

A green delight featuring spinach and broccoli, accompanied by Swiss chard and arugula.

Nutritional Information (per serving):
Calories: 80 kcal | Carbohydrates: 9g | Protein: 5g | Fat: 4g

INGREDIENTS:
- 100g spinach
- 100g broccoli florets
- 100g Swiss chard
- 100g arugula
- 1 onion, chopped
- 2 cloves garlic, minced
- 1 litre vegetable broth
- Fresh parsley leaves (for garnish)

INSTRUCTIONS:
1. Place spinach, broccoli florets, Swiss chard, arugula, chopped onion, and minced garlic in the soup maker.
2. Add vegetable broth and let it simmer until the greens are tender.
3. Serve hot, garnished with fresh parsley leaves.

7. SPRING GREENS AND ASPARAGUS SOUP

A spring-inspired soup featuring an array of greens: spinach, watercress, arugula, and asparagus.

Nutritional Information (per serving):
Calories: 85 kcal | Carbohydrates: 10g | Protein: 5g | Fat: 4g

INGREDIENTS:

- 100g spinach
- 100g watercress
- 100g arugula
- 100g asparagus, chopped
- 1 leek, chopped
- 2 cloves garlic, minced
- 1 litre vegetable broth
- Fresh basil leaves (for garnish)

INSTRUCTIONS:

1 Place spinach, watercress, arugula, chopped asparagus, chopped leek, and minced garlic in the soup maker.

2 Add vegetable broth and let it simmer until the greens are tender.

3 Serve hot, garnished with fresh basil leaves.

8. MIXED GREENS AND PEAS SOUP

A vibrant green soup featuring a mix of greens including spinach, kale, mustard greens, and peas.

Nutritional Information (per serving):
Calories: 75 kcal | Carbohydrates: 10g | Protein: 4g | Fat: 3g

INGREDIENTS:

- 100g spinach
- 100g kale
- 100g mustard greens
- 100g peas (fresh or frozen)
- 1 onion, chopped
- 2 cloves garlic, minced
- 1 litre vegetable broth
- Fresh thyme leaves (for garnish)

INSTRUCTIONS:

1 Place spinach, kale, mustard greens, peas, chopped onion, and minced garlic in the soup maker.

2 Add vegetable broth and let it simmer until the greens are tender.

3 Serve hot, garnished with fresh thyme leaves.

9. HEARTY GREENS AND LENTIL SOUP

A hearty and nutritious soup featuring a medley of greens: spinach, Swiss chard, collard greens, and lentils.

Nutritional Information (per serving):
Calories: 90 kcal | Carbohydrates: 12g | Protein: 6g | Fat: 3g

INGREDIENTS:

- 100g spinach
- 100g Swiss chard
- 100g collard greens
- 100g green or brown lentils
- 1 onion, chopped
- 2 cloves garlic, minced
- 1 litre vegetable broth
- Fresh rosemary leaves (for garnish)

INSTRUCTIONS:

1 Place spinach, Swiss chard, collard greens, lentils, chopped onion, and minced garlic in the soup maker.

2 Add vegetable broth and let it simmer until the greens and lentils are tender.

3 Serve hot, garnished with fresh rosemary leaves.

10. TRIPLE GREEN PEA AND MINT SOUP

A refreshing green soup featuring three types of greens: spinach, peas, and fresh mint.

Nutritional Information (per serving):
Calories: 70 kcal | Carbohydrates: 10g | Protein: 4g | Fat: 3g

INGREDIENTS:

- 100g spinach
- 100g green peas (fresh or frozen)
- 100g sugar snap peas
- 1 onion, chopped
- 2 cloves garlic, minced
- 1 litre vegetable broth
- Fresh mint leaves (for garnish)

INSTRUCTIONS:

1 Place spinach, green peas, sugar snap peas, chopped onion, and minced garlic in the soup maker.

2 Add vegetable broth and let it simmer until the greens and peas are tender.

3 Serve hot, garnished with fresh mint leaves.

11. FOUR GREENS AND COURGETTE SOUP

A garden-fresh soup featuring spinach, Swiss chard, arugula, and courgette.

Nutritional Information (per serving):
Calories: 75 kcal | Carbohydrates: 9g | Protein: 4g | Fat: 4g

INGREDIENTS:

- 100g spinach
- 100g Swiss chard
- 100g arugula
- 100g courgette, chopped
- 1 onion, chopped
- 2 cloves garlic, minced
- 1 litre vegetable broth
- Fresh dill leaves (for garnish)

INSTRUCTIONS:

1 Place spinach, Swiss chard, arugula, chopped courgette, chopped onion, and minced garlic in the soup maker.

2 Add vegetable broth and let it simmer until the greens and courgette are tender.

3 Serve hot, garnished with fresh dill leaves.

12. GREEN CURRY AND BOK CHOY SOUP

A vibrant and spicy green curry soup featuring baby bok choy, spinach, and watercress.

Nutritional Information (per serving):
Calories: 90 kcal | Carbohydrates: 11g | Protein: 5g | Fat: 4g

INGREDIENTS:

- 100g baby bok choy
- 100g spinach
- 100g watercress
- 2 tbsps green curry paste
- 1 can (400ml) coconut milk
- 1 litre vegetable broth
- Fresh coriander leaves (for garnish)

INSTRUCTIONS:

1 Place baby bok choy, spinach, watercress, and green curry paste in the soup maker.

2 Add coconut milk and vegetable broth, and let it simmer until the greens are tender.

3 Serve hot, garnished with fresh coriander leaves.

13. MIXED GREENS AND FENNEL SOUP

A fresh and aromatic green soup featuring a mix of greens along with the delightful flavour of fennel.

Nutritional Information (per serving):
Calories: 80 kcal | Carbohydrates: 10g | Protein: 4g | Fat: 3g

INGREDIENTS:

- 100g spinach
- 100g kale
- 100g fennel bulb, sliced
- 100g dandelion greens (or other wild greens)
- 1 onion, chopped
- 2 cloves garlic, minced
- 1 litre vegetable broth
- Fresh tarragon leaves (for garnish)

INSTRUCTIONS:

1 Place spinach, kale, sliced fennel, dandelion greens, chopped onion, and minced garlic in the soup maker.

2 Add vegetable broth and let it simmer until the greens and fennel are tender.

3 Serve hot, garnished with fresh tarragon leaves.

14. GARDEN GREENS AND AVOCADO SOUP

A creamy and refreshing green soup featuring spinach, arugula, watercress, and creamy avocado.

Nutritional Information (per serving):
Calories: 85 kcal | Carbohydrates: 9g | Protein: 4g | Fat: 5g

INGREDIENTS:

- 100g spinach
- 100g arugula
- 100g watercress
- 1 avocado, peeled and chopped
- 1 onion, chopped
- 2 cloves garlic, minced
- 1 litre vegetable broth
- Fresh chives (for garnish)

INSTRUCTIONS:

1 Place spinach, arugula, watercress, chopped avocado, chopped onion, and minced garlic in the soup maker.

2 Add vegetable broth and let it simmer until the greens and avocado are tender.

3 Serve hot, garnished with fresh chives.

15. MEDITERRANEAN GREENS AND TOMATO SOUP

A Mediterranean-inspired green soup featuring spinach, Swiss chard, collard greens, and flavorful tomatoes.

Nutritional Information (per serving):
Calories: 80 kcal | Carbohydrates: 10g | Protein: 4g | Fat: 4g

INGREDIENTS:
- 100g spinach
- 100g Swiss chard
- 100g collard greens
- 250ml cherry tomatoes, halved
- 1 onion, chopped
- 2 cloves garlic, minced
- 1 litre vegetable broth
- Fresh basil leaves (for garnish)

INSTRUCTIONS:
1 Place spinach, Swiss chard, collard greens, halved cherry tomatoes, chopped onion, and minced garlic in the soup maker.

2 Add vegetable broth and let it simmer until the greens and tomatoes are tender.

3 Serve hot, garnished with fresh basil leaves.

16. ASIAN GREENS AND TOFU SOUP

An Asian-inspired green soup featuring a mix of greens, tofu, and aromatic spices.

Nutritional Information (per serving):
Calories: 90 kcal | Carbohydrates: 11g | Protein: 6g | Fat: 4g

INGREDIENTS:
- 100g spinach
- 100g bok choy
- 100g mustard greens
- 100g tofu, cubed
- 1 onion, chopped
- 2 cloves garlic, minced
- 1 litre vegetable broth
- Fresh coriander leaves (for garnish)

INSTRUCTIONS:
1 Place spinach, bok choy, mustard greens, cubed tofu, chopped onion, and minced garlic in the soup maker.

2 Add vegetable broth and let it simmer until the greens and tofu are tender.

3 Serve hot, garnished with fresh coriander leaves.

17. PEPPERY GREENS AND POTATO SOUP

A peppery and hearty green soup featuring spinach, arugula, watercress, and creamy potatoes.

Nutritional Information (per serving):
Calories: 85 kcal | Carbohydrates: 10g | Protein: 4g | Fat: 4g

INGREDIENTS:

- 100g spinach
- 100g arugula
- 100g watercress
- 200g potatoes, peeled and diced
- 1 onion, chopped
- 2 cloves garlic, minced
- 1 litre vegetable broth
- Fresh thyme leaves (for garnish)

INSTRUCTIONS:

1 Place spinach, arugula, watercress, diced potatoes, chopped onion, and minced garlic in the soup maker.

2 Add vegetable broth and let it simmer until the greens and potatoes are tender.

3 Serve hot, garnished with fresh thyme leaves.

18. CREAMY BROCCOLI AND GREEN BEAN SOUP

A creamy and green soup featuring broccoli, green beans, spinach, and arugula.

Nutritional Information (per serving):
Calories: 90 kcal | Carbohydrates: 10g | Protein: 4g | Fat: 4g

INGREDIENTS:

- 100g broccoli florets
- 100g green beans, trimmed and chopped
- 100g spinach
- 100g arugula
- 1 onion, chopped
- 2 cloves garlic, minced
- 1 litre vegetable broth
- Fresh chervil leaves (for garnish)

INSTRUCTIONS:

1 Place broccoli florets, chopped green beans, spinach, arugula, chopped onion, and minced garlic in the soup maker.

2 Add vegetable broth and let it simmer until the greens and vegetables are tender.

3 Serve hot, garnished with fresh chervil leaves.

19. CREAMY SPINACH AND COURGETTE BLOSSOM SOUP

A creamy and delicate green soup featuring spinach, courgette blossoms, and a touch of nutmeg.

Nutritional Information (per serving):
Calories: 85 kcal | Carbohydrates: 10g | Protein: 4g | Fat: 4g

INGREDIENTS:
- 100g spinach
- 100g courgette blossoms, chopped
- 100g Swiss chard
- 1 courgette, chopped
- 1 onion, chopped
- 2 cloves garlic, minced
- 1 litre vegetable broth
- Fresh nutmeg (for garnish)

INSTRUCTIONS:
1. Place spinach, chopped courgette blossoms, Swiss chard, chopped courgette, chopped onion, and minced garlic in the soup maker.
2. Add vegetable broth and let it simmer until the greens and courgette are tender.
3. Serve hot, garnished with freshly grated nutmeg.

20. SPICY GREENS AND CHICKPEA SOUP

A spicy and protein-packed green soup featuring a mix of greens, chickpeas, and bold spices.

Nutritional Information (per serving):
Calories: 100 kcal | Carbohydrates: 12g | Protein: 6g | Fat: 4g

INGREDIENTS:
- 100g spinach
- 100g arugula
- 100g Swiss chard
- 100g chickpeas (canned or cooked)
- 1 onion, chopped
- 2 cloves garlic, minced
- 1 litre vegetable broth
- Fresh coriander leaves (for garnish)

INSTRUCTIONS:
1. Place spinach, arugula, Swiss chard, chickpeas, chopped onion, and minced garlic in the soup maker.
2. Add vegetable broth and let it simmer until the greens and chickpeas are tender.
3. Serve hot, garnished with fresh coriander leaves.

NON-SOUP RECIPES FOR SOUP MAKERS

The soup maker, with its ingenious design and multifunctional prowess, is not limited to crafting just soups. While it excels in melding flavours for heartwarming broths and stews, this versatile device is equally adept at conjuring a range of non-soup delicacies, opening doors to a myriad of culinary possibilities.

In this chapter, we'll venture beyond the conventional, exploring the lesser-trodden path of non-soup recipes that can be masterfully executed in a soup maker. From creamy smoothies and rich sauces to velvety purees and even steamy lattes, the scope is vast and excitingly uncharted.

Picture a silky chocolate fondue, perfect for a romantic evening, or a vibrant berry compote to drizzle over your morning pancakes. The convenience and efficiency of the soup maker mean these dishes, which might typically demand various appliances, can be whipped up with minimal fuss and maximum flavour.

Step with us into this innovative culinary space, where boundaries are redefined and creativity knows no bounds. Whether you're seeking to diversify your menu, save on kitchen space, or simply surprise your guests, this chapter promises a treasure trove of unconventional recipes tailored for the humble soup maker.

1. CREAMY STRAWBERRY ICE CREAM

Indulge in homemade strawberry ice cream made effortlessly in your soup maker.

INGREDIENTS:

- 500g frozen strawberries
- 300ml condensed milk
- 300ml heavy cream

INSTRUCTIONS:

1 Place frozen strawberries, condensed milk, and heavy cream in the soup maker.

2 Blend until smooth and creamy.

3 Freeze the mixture for a few hours before serving.

2. CHOCOLATE FONDUE

Prepare a delightful chocolate fondue for dipping fruits, marshmallows, and more.

INGREDIENTS:

- 200g dark chocolate, chopped
- 200ml heavy cream
- 1 tsp vanilla extract
- Assorted dippers (strawberries, bananas, marshmallows, etc.)

INSTRUCTIONS:

1 Place chopped dark chocolate, heavy cream, and vanilla extract in the soup maker.

2 Heat on low until the chocolate is fully melted and the mixture is smooth.

3 Serve with your favourite dippers.

3. LEMON CURD

Make tangy and zesty lemon curd for spreading on toast or using as a dessert topping.

INGREDIENTS:

- 4 large lemons, zest and juice
- 200g sugar
- 100g unsalted butter
- 4 large eggs

INSTRUCTIONS:

1 Place lemon zest, lemon juice, sugar, and unsalted butter in the soup maker.
2 Heat until the butter melts and the sugar dissolves.
3 In a separate bowl, whisk the eggs and gradually add the hot lemon mixture while whisking.
4 Return the mixture to the soup maker and heat until it thickens.
5 Allow to cool before using.

4. CHAI TEA LATTE

Create a comforting chai tea latte infused with spices and creamy milk.

INGREDIENTS:

- 2 black tea bags
- 1 litre water
- 1 cinnamon stick
- 4 cloves
- 4 cardamom pods
- 4 black peppercorns
- 250ml milk
- Honey or sugar (to taste)

INSTRUCTIONS:

1 Place black tea bags, water, cinnamon stick, cloves, cardamom pods, and black peppercorns in the soup maker.
2 Heat until it simmers, then add milk and sweetener.
3 Allow it to steep for a few minutes before serving.

5. PUMPKIN SPICE LATTE

Enjoy a homemade pumpkin spice latte with the perfect blend of pumpkin and warm spices.

INGREDIENTS:

- 250ml brewed coffee
- 1/2 cup milk
- 2 tbsps pumpkin puree
- 2 tbsps sugar
- 1/2 tsp pumpkin pie spice
- Whipped cream (optional)

INSTRUCTIONS:

1 Combine brewed coffee, milk, pumpkin puree, sugar, and pumpkin pie spice in the soup maker.

2 Heat and whisk until well combined.

3 Serve with whipped cream, if desired.

6. MANGO SORBET

Cool down with a refreshing mango sorbet that's easy to make.

INGREDIENTS:

- 500g frozen mango chunks
- 100ml orange juice
- 50g honey or sugar (adjust to taste)

INSTRUCTIONS:

1 Place frozen mango chunks, orange juice, and honey (or sugar) in the soup maker.

2 Blend until smooth.

3 Freeze for a few hours to firm up before serving.

7. RICE PUDDING

Create a creamy and comforting rice pudding with minimal effort.

INGREDIENTS:

- 250ml Arborio rice
- 1 litre milk
- 1/2 cup sugar
- 1 tsp vanilla extract
- Ground cinnamon (for garnish)

INSTRUCTIONS:

1 Place Arborio rice, milk, sugar, and vanilla extract in the soup maker.

2 Cook until the rice is tender and the mixture is creamy.

3 Serve warm or chilled, garnished with ground cinnamon.

8. APPLE CIDER

Prepare a warm and spiced apple cider perfect for chilly evenings.

INGREDIENTS:

- 1 litre apple juice or cider
- 2 cinnamon sticks
- 4 cloves
- 4 allspice berries
- 1 orange, sliced

INSTRUCTIONS:

1. Combine apple juice or cider, cinnamon sticks, cloves, allspice berries, and orange slices in the soup maker.
2. Heat until warm and aromatic.
3. Serve hot.

9. BLUEBERRY COMPOTE

Make a delicious blueberry compote for topping pancakes, yogurt, or ice cream.

INGREDIENTS:

- 500ml fresh or frozen blueberries
- 1/2 cup sugar
- 2 tbsps lemon juice
- 1 tsp cornstarch (optional, for thickening)

INSTRUCTIONS:

1. Place blueberries, sugar, lemon juice, and cornstarch (if using) in the soup maker.
2. Cook until the blueberries burst and the mixture thickens.
3. Allow to cool before using.

10. CARAMEL SAUCE

Craft a rich and buttery caramel sauce to drizzle over desserts.

INGREDIENTS:

- 250ml sugar
- 1/4 cup water
- 1/2 cup heavy cream
- 2 tbsps unsalted butter
- 1 tsp vanilla extract

INSTRUCTIONS:

1 Place sugar and water in the soup maker.

2 Heat until the mixture turns golden brown.

3 Carefully add heavy cream, unsalted butter, and vanilla extract while stirring.

4 Continue to cook until smooth and creamy.

5 Allow to cool before using.

11. HOT CHOCOLATE

Prepare a velvety and indulgent hot chocolate to warm your soul.

INGREDIENTS:

- 1 litre milk
- 200g semisweet chocolate, chopped
- 2 tbsps cocoa powder
- 2 tbsps sugar
- Whipped cream and chocolate shavings (for garnish)

INSTRUCTIONS:

1 Combine milk, chopped semisweet chocolate, cocoa powder, and sugar in the soup maker.

2 Heat until the chocolate is melted and the mixture is smooth.

3 Serve hot with whipped cream and chocolate shavings.

12. SPICED PEAR TEA

Sip on a fragrant spiced pear tea with the sweetness of ripe pears and aromatic spices.

INGREDIENTS:

- 4 ripe pears, peeled and chopped
- 1 litre water
- 1 cinnamon stick
- 4 cloves
- Honey (to taste)

INSTRUCTIONS:

1 Place chopped ripe pears, water, cinnamon stick, and cloves in the soup maker.

2 Heat until the pears are tender and the flavours meld.

3 Sweeten with honey to taste before serving.

13. CHOCOLATE PEANUT BUTTER SMOOTHIE

Whip up a creamy and protein-packed chocolate peanut butter smoothie.

INGREDIENTS:

- 2 ripe bananas
- 2 tbsps cocoa powder
- 2 tbsps peanut butter
- 500ml milk (or dairy-free alternative)
- Honey or maple syrup (to taste)

INSTRUCTIONS:

1 Combine ripe bananas, cocoa powder, peanut butter, milk, and sweetener in the soup maker.

2 Blend until smooth and creamy.

3 Serve chilled.

14. LAVENDER AND HONEY INFUSED TEA

Relax with a soothing lavender and honey-infused tea.

INGREDIENTS:

- 1 litre water
- 2 tbsps dried lavender buds
- Honey (to taste)
- Fresh lavender sprigs (for garnish)

INSTRUCTIONS:

1 Place dried lavender buds and water in the soup maker.

2 Heat until the lavender infuses into the water.

3 Sweeten with honey to taste and garnish with fresh lavender sprigs.

15. PUMPKIN PIE SMOOTHIE

Enjoy the flavours of fall with a pumpkin pie-inspired smoothie.

INGREDIENTS:

- 250ml canned pumpkin puree
- 250ml milk (or dairy-free alternative)
- 1/2 cup plain yogurt
- 2 tbsps maple syrup
- 1/2 tsp pumpkin pie spice
- Whipped cream and cinnamon (for garnish)

INSTRUCTIONS:

1 Combine canned pumpkin puree, milk, plain yogurt, maple syrup, and pumpkin pie spice in the soup maker.

2 Blend until smooth.

3 Serve with whipped cream and a sprinkle of cinnamon.

16. MATCHA GREEN TEA LATTE

Savour the earthy and vibrant flavours of matcha in a latte.

INGREDIENTS:

- 2 tsp matcha green tea powder
- 500ml milk (or dairy-free alternative)
- 2 tbsp honey or sweetener (adjust to taste)

INSTRUCTIONS:

1 Whisk matcha green tea powder, milk, and sweetener in the soup maker.
2 Heat until well combined and frothy.
3 Serve hot.

17. RASPBERRY JAM

Make homemade raspberry jam to spread on toast, scones, or desserts.

INGREDIENTS:

- 500g fresh raspberries
- 300g sugar
- 1 lemon, juice and zest

INSTRUCTIONS:

1 Place fresh raspberries, sugar, lemon juice, and zest in the soup maker.
2 Heat until the raspberries break down and the mixture thickens.
3 Allow to cool before using.

18. VANILLA RICE MILK

Create a dairy-free vanilla rice milk for a delicious and versatile beverage.

INGREDIENTS:

- 250ml cooked rice
- 1 litre water
- 2 tsps vanilla extract
- 2 tbsps sugar (adjust to taste)

INSTRUCTIONS:

1 Blend cooked rice, water, vanilla extract, and sugar in the soup maker.
2 Heat until well combined.
3 Serve chilled.

19. MINT CHOCOLATE CHIP MILKSHAKE

Blend up a cool and refreshing mint chocolate chip milkshake.

INGREDIENTS:
- 500ml vanilla ice cream
- 250ml milk (or dairy-free alternative)
- 1/2 tsp peppermint extract
- 1/2 cup chocolate chips
- Fresh mint leaves (for garnish)

INSTRUCTIONS:
1 Combine vanilla ice cream, milk, peppermint extract, and chocolate chips in the soup maker.
2 Blend until smooth.
3 Serve with fresh mint leaves.

20. GINGER AND LEMON IMMUNITY TEA

Boost your immunity with a warming ginger and lemon tea.

INGREDIENTS:
- 1 litre water
- 1-inch piece of fresh ginger, sliced
- Juice of 1 lemon
- Honey (to taste)

INSTRUCTIONS:
1 Place fresh ginger slices and water in the soup maker.
2 Heat until the ginger infuses into the water.
3 Stir in lemon juice and sweeten with honey to taste before serving.

SUMMARY

"The XXL Soup Maker Recipe Book" is a comprehensive culinary guide that explores the limitless possibilities of creating delicious soups using a soup maker. With an extensive collection of over 100 recipes, this book offers a diverse range of soup options, from classic favourites to exotic international flavours, ensuring that there's something for every palate and occasion.

The book begins by introducing readers to the world of soup makers, emphasising the benefits of these kitchen appliances. It highlights the time-saving convenience, effortless operation, and versatility of soup makers, making them a must-have tool for both novice and experienced cooks. Additionally, the book underscores the advantages of healthier eating and cost-effective meal preparation when using a soup maker.

The heart of the book lies in its vast collection of soup recipes. These recipes are meticulously organised, providing readers with a user-friendly format that includes a recipe number, a succinct description, nutritional information per serving (calories, carbohydrates, protein, and fat), a list of ingredients, and step-by-step instructions. Each recipe is tailored to the capabilities of a soup maker, ensuring that the cooking process is efficient and hassle-free.

The recipes span a wide spectrum of flavours and ingredients, catering to various dietary preferences and culinary interests. From hearty classics like Creamy Chicken and Potato Soup to exotic international creations like Thai Coconut Curry Soup, the book takes readers on a global culinary journey. Special dietary needs are also considered, with options for vegetarian, vegan, gluten-free, and dairy-free soups.

The book doesn't stop at traditional savoury soups. It extends its culinary exploration to include unconventional but delectable recipes that demonstrate the versatility of a soup maker. These include recipes for making ice cream, desserts, teas, and various beverages. Whether you're craving a Creamy Strawberry Ice Cream or a soothing Chai Tea Latte, this book has you covered.

To help readers become proficient soup makers, the book provides detailed guidance on the basic operation of these appliances. It offers step-by-step instructions, from ingredient preparation to selecting the right program on the soup maker. With these instructions, even those new to soup making can achieve culinary success.

In summary, "The XXL Soup Maker Recipe Book" is a comprehensive and user-friendly resource that empowers readers to make the most of their soup makers. With a wide array of soup recipes, along with unconventional treats and beverages, this book caters to all tastes and occasions. Whether you're seeking comfort, adventure, or convenience in the kitchen, this cookbook is your go-to guide for creating delicious soups and more with ease. So, embrace your inner chef, unleash your creativity, and embark on a culinary journey that promises to delight your taste buds and simplify your cooking experience.

DISCLAIMER

The XXL Soup Maker Recipe Book is intended solely for informational and entertainment purposes. While every effort has been made to ensure the accuracy and completeness of the recipes and information contained within this book, we cannot guarantee the outcome of any recipe or the safety of any cooking methods used.

Cooking involves inherent risks, including but not limited to burns, cuts, allergies, and foodborne illnesses. The author, publisher, and any affiliated individuals or organizations shall not be held responsible for any injuries, losses, or damages that may result from the use of this book or the recipes contained within it.

Readers are advised to exercise caution and common sense when preparing recipes from this book. Always follow proper food safety guidelines, including the handling and storage of ingredients, and consult with a qualified healthcare professional or nutritionist if you have any dietary restrictions, allergies, or specific health concerns.

Additionally, the nutritional information provided in this book is intended as a general guideline and should not be considered a substitute for professional medical advice. Individual nutritional needs may vary, and readers are encouraged to consult with a healthcare professional or registered dietitian for personalized dietary recommendations.

By using this book and its recipes, readers acknowledge and accept the inherent risks associated with cooking and understand that they are responsible for their own safety and well-being. The author and publisher disclaim any liability for any consequences that may arise from the use of this book or the recipes it contains.

Please cook responsibly and enjoy the delicious and nutritious recipes in this book with care and consideration for your own health and safety.

EXCLUSIVE BONUS

40 Weight Loss Recipes

&

14 Days Meal Plan

Scan the QR-Code and receive
the FREE download:

Printed in Great Britain
by Amazon

32883030R00088